HAWAIIAN QUILT MASTERPIECES

HAWAIIAN QUILT MASTERPIECES

Robert Shaw

UNIVERSE

Published by
Universe Publishing,
A Division of Rizzoli International Publications, Inc.
300 Park Avenue South
New York, NY 10010
www.rizzoliusa.com

© 2009 Universe Publishing

Design: Ken Scaglia
Photo Research: Ellin Y. Silberblatt
Editorial Production: Deborah Teipel Zindell

2009 2010 2011 2012 / 10 9 8 7 6 5 4 3 2 1

Printed in China

ISBN-13: 978-0-7893-9963-2

Library of Congress Catalog Control Number: 2008933175

Contents

Acknowledgments

This book benefitted enormously from the assistance of many generous friends, some old, some new, in Hawaii. Foremost among these was Elizabeth Akana, who warmly encouraged me from the start, suggested several remarkable quilts for inclusion, arranged new photography, contacted other quilters, and read the introduction with a critical eye. Elaine Zinn also read the introduction and offered a number of important suggestions for improvement. Lee Wild sent information about contemporary quiltmakers, assessed the physical condition of several antique quilts, and helped with new photography of quilts owned by the Daughters of Hawaii. Deborah Dunn of the Mission Houses Museum was responsible for the photography of some of their most important quilts. Loretta Woodard and other members of the Hawaiian Quilt Research Project provided updated information about the group and its activities. Sharon Balai, Helen Friend, Junedale Quinories, and Stan Yates contributed detailed information about their work and experiences. Many other island quilters sent photos of their work for consideration; I am indebted to them all for helping me to understand contemporary Hawaiian quiltmaking.

On the mainland, Joel Kopp of America Hurrah in New York graciously lent his copy of Stella Jones's book and alerted us to several quilts and historic photos. In San Francisco, Sharon Risedorph took beautiful pictures of a number of previously unphotographed quilts.

I am, as always, extremely grateful to Hugh Levin, who suggested the project and supported it from start to finish, and to my ever patient, tenacious colleague, editor Ellin Silberblatt, who kept the book moving steadily forward through innumerable small setbacks and called Hawaii even more often than I did. Thanks also to text editor Debby Zindell, who improved the manuscript in a thousand ways, and to Ken Scaglia, who provided the book's graceful design.

Finally, loving thanks to my girls: my daughters Emma and Georgia and my wife Nancy, who joined me in dreams of paradise all through a long, cold, snowy New England winter.

Robert Shaw
Shelburne, Vermont

Introduction

QUILTS IN PARADISE

Hawaii's quilts, more than those of any other region or people, are intimately connected with place. They directly reflect the history and natural world of the islands where they were made, and the culture and beliefs of the people who made them. Born of the collision of British, American, and traditional Hawaiian cultures after the islands' discovery in the late 1700s, Hawaiian quilts evoke the spirit of a legendary and universally coveted island paradise and are emblems of the islands' continually evolving struggle to maintain their identity and integrity in the face of the powerful homogenizing forces of international tourism, immigration, and development. Although bedcovers were not needed for warmth in Hawaii's balmy climate, islanders found the creative, decorative, and expressive possibilities of quiltmaking irresistible. They blended elements of their Polynesian heritage with the American quilt, creating a unique synthesis that expresses the essence of the islands perfectly. Hawaii's quilts are as distinctive and beautiful as the land that produced them, an art form that embodies both the islands' stunning natural beauty and its people's beguiling grace and charm.

Situated squarely in the middle of the vast Pacific Ocean, over 2,400 miles away from the nearest continental land mass, the Hawaiian Islands are the most geographically remote group of islands in the world. They are volcanic in origin, in effect mountaintops that were lifted out of the sea by the buildup of molten rock spewed out over millions of years of intermittent but intense volcanic activity. These explosions eventually built a range of enormous undersea mountains. Indeed, when measured from its base on the ocean floor, Mauna Kea on the island of Hawaii is the world's tallest peak, rising 19,686 feet to reach sea level and another 13,796 feet above the island to its snow-capped summit. Volcanic activity continues to reshape the landscape and geography of the islands to the present day: two volcanoes on the island of Hawaii are active, and scientists have detected an undersea volcano slowly building a new island to its south.

Hawaii is an archipelago, a chain of 132 islands, atolls, and shoals spread across some 1,600 miles of ocean. The majority of these are mere specks of land, tiny, barren, and uninhabited. Only six of the islands, all located within 300 miles of each other at the southern end of the chain, are large enough to support populations of any size. The largest and most recently formed island is Hawaii itself, the so-called Big Island, which is located at the extreme southeast end of the chain. Its 4,038 square miles make it several times the size of its nearest competitor and nearly twice the size of all 131 others combined. To Hawaii's northwest is Maui, which is closely ringed by the smaller satellite islands of Kahoolawe and Lanai to the west and Molokai to the north. (Tiny Kahoolawe,

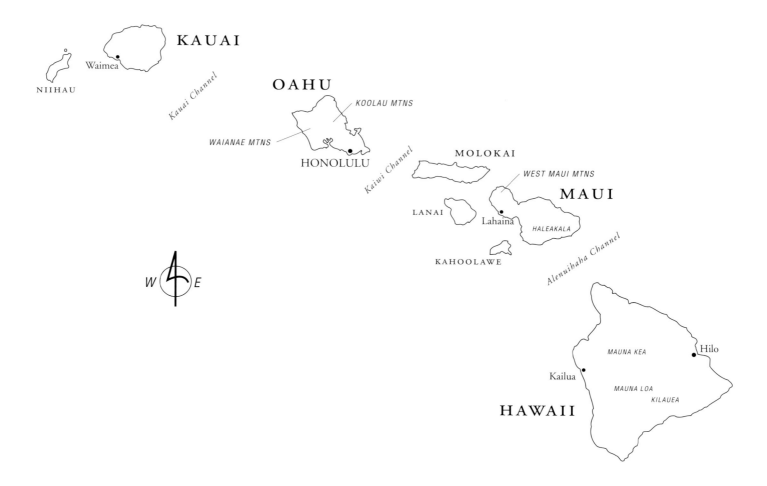

only 45 miles square, is uninhabited and was for many years used as a target range by the U.S. Army and Navy.) Oahu, the island of Honolulu, Diamond Head, Waikiki, and Pearl Harbor, as well as nearly half of Hawaii's population and 85 percent of its tourists, and Kauai, similar in size to Maui, follow to the northwest. The group of major islands is completed by the small (73 square miles), privately owned, and sparsely populated island of Niihau, just west of Kauai.

Before human habitation of the islands, Hawaii's extreme geographical isolation and lush tropical climate helped to create a unique natural world full of flora and fauna found nowhere else on Earth. Because the islands were originally no more than bare volcanic rock, plants and animals, like the people who would arrive much later, came to Hawaii from faraway lands. A few birds and insects flew the great distances, and some seeds were carried by the birds or blown by the winds. Most land-based reptiles, amphibians, and mammals could not travel the great expanses of open water; only the monk seal and one species of bat arrived without help from man. The new arrivals evolved in an environment far removed from the influence of the outside world, mutating over time from a small number of long-distance travelers into hundreds of unique new species.

The islands are believed to have been first discovered and settled around A.D. 400 by venturesome Polynesian sailors from the Marquesas Islands, over 2,400 miles of open ocean away. Traveling in sixty- to eighty-foot-long double-hulled canoes, the remarkable early mariners of Polynesia sailed throughout the South Pacific in search of other inhabitable lands. Wherever the Polynesians sailed, they carried their culture and way of life, transplanting their polytheistic religion and chief-ruled social structure along with the breadfruit, coconuts, pineapples, taro, bananas, sweet potatoes, yams, dogs, chickens, and pigs that traveled with them in their canoes. Hawaii was the last group of islands discovered and colonized by these voyagers, who had begun to explore and spread their civilization some two thousand years earlier.

The Hawaiian Islands' remote location also fostered cultural isolation. They remained unknown to and uninfluenced by either the Western or Oriental world for over thirteen hundred years after their settlement by the Polynesians, although a second group of migrants from Tahiti arrived around A.D. 1300. In addition to the singular ecology of the islands, they became home to a rich human culture during their millennium of isolation. The islanders, influenced by their Polynesian heritage, were also shaped by their unique environment, evolving a complex but unwritten language, their own set of gods, and a hierarchical society ruled by omnipotent kings. Hawaii's isolation from the outside world finally ended in 1778, when the British explorer Captain James Cook landed on what he called the Sandwich Islands, named after one of his patrons, the Earl of Sandwich. Soon after Cook's discovery, the islands were mapped, and within a few years other foreign navigators began to visit on a regular basis.

New England missionaries first arrived in Hawaii in 1820 and maintained schools in the islands for much of the nineteenth century. For many years, it was thought that the women of the islands first learned quiltmaking in these missionary schools. Although missionaries certainly played a major role in the evolution of the Hawaiian quilt, it now appears that establishing the origins of quiltmaking in Hawaii is far more complex. The missionaries probably did bring the first American quilts to the islands, and they did teach their methods of sewing to Hawaiian women and children. What is not clear is exactly how and from whom the natives learned to make their own distinctive quilts, which, in both technique and design, are quite different from those of any mainland tradition.

Hawaiians knew how to sew and work with cloth long before the Americans and Europeans arrived. For centuries before cotton and other natural fibers and finished woven cloths were introduced to the islands, Hawaiians had made their own cloth, called *tapa*, from the bark of the paper mulberry tree. Tapa (often spelled *kapa* today) was created by pounding thin sheets of the inner bark of the paper mulberry together with wooden mallets to form larger, thicker, and stronger pieces of bark cloth. From tapa, which could be sewn with bird bones or native hardwood needles and thread twisted from bits of natural bark fiber, the islanders made clothing and bedding as well as ceremonial flags and streamers for the masts of their outrigger canoes. After being pounded to the desired thickness, tapa could be colored with natural dyes and decorated with designs, which were drawn freehand with penlike instruments and were usually based on natural forms. Bed coverings made from tapa were called *kapa moe*, a name that Hawaiians later applied to their cloth quilts. *Kapa moe* were made by joining together several layers of white tapa with long, loose running stitches of thread. Like a quilt top, the top layer of *kapa moe* was usually colored and/or decorated. The concept of multilayered, decorated bedcovers was, therefore, not new to Hawaiians, who likened their bark cloth *kapa moe* to quilts brought by American and European visitors and immigrants.

In her diary, Lucy Thurston, wife of one of the first missionaries to come to the islands, tells of the initial encounter between missionaries who had sailed from Boston as passengers on the brig *Thaddeus* and a group of high-ranking Hawaiians who had come to greet the ship on its arrival and accompany the missionaries to see the king. Among the dignitaries was Kalakua, the queen dowager, who was, by all accounts, a woman of ample proportions. Thurston recalled that "Kalakua brought a web of white cambric to have a dress made for herself in the fashion of our ladies, and was very particular in her wish to have it finished while sailing along the western side of the island, before reaching the king . . . Monday morning April 3rd [1820], the first sewing circle was formed that the sun ever looked down upon in this Hawaiian realm. Kalakua was directress. She requested all the seven white ladies to take seats with them on mats, on the deck of the *Thaddeus.* Mrs. Holman and Mrs. Ruggles were executive officers to ply the scissors and prepare the work . . . The four native women of distinction were furnished with calico patchwork to sew—a new employment to them."

The early quilt researcher Stella Jones, who published the first history of island quiltmaking in 1930, assumed that Mrs. Thurston and her companions were teaching the Hawaiians to make patchwork quilts, and most of the subsequent histories have accepted Jones's interpretation. However, the report bears further scrutiny for at least two important reasons. First, in 1820 the words *patchwork, quilting,* and *quiltmaking* were not necessarily synonymous. Patchwork, the stitching together of a number of small pieces of fabric to form a larger textile, was often used as a way to teach sewing; all patchwork did not necessarily become part of a quilt. Second, quilts made entirely of patchwork were rare in 1820. Whole cloth and central medallion quilts were the preferred formats at the time in both America and Europe, and while central medallions sometimes included some patchwork, appliquéd medallions were far more common. The development of the block-style pieced quilt that later dominated American quiltmaking was in its infancy. It seems likely, therefore, that Lucy Thurston's "sewing circle," as she called it, was not the instructional quilting bee that Stella Jones envisioned, but was, rather, simply intended to introduce the Hawaiians to American

domestic arts and, perhaps more important, keep them occupied. The point is further supported by the fact that, with only a handful of exceptions, early Hawaiians simply do not seem to have made pieced quilts. Stella Jones speculated that the idea of piecing—cutting cloth into pieces to then be sewn back together—seemed nonsensical to the Hawaiians, who chose to appliqué their quilts instead. This may or may not be true. Whatever the reason, almost all the evidence now leads to the conclusion that nineteenth-century Hawaiian quilts were, almost without exception, appliquéd, and that they were appliquéd from the first.

Writing in *The Islands,* W. Storrs Lee relates that "The favorite benevolence of the home missionary society was . . . an 'album quilt' with the signatures of the seamstresses stitched into the squares. The names constituted a kind of endorsement, and though nothing was much more useless in Hawaii . . . , they were prized possessions." These presentation album quilts, which like most album quilts were probably made up of appliquéd squares, were most likely seen by the Hawaiians and may have been the models for teaching in the missionary schools. Samuel Chapman Armstrong, who grew up to become a general and the founder of Virginia's Hampton Institute, was the son of a missionary and recalled his days in the 1850s as a young student in "Mrs. Rice's sewing class, where we made quilts for the Oregon Indians." This was, of course, a perfectly acceptable missionary activity in a climate where quilts were not needed. And, like the presentation quilts of the home missionary service, these charitable quilts were almost certainly made collectively, with each student working on a square. Armstrong recalled

Kihapai Pua O Kauai (The Garden Island of Kauai). Artist unknown. c. 1915. Kauai.
Cottons, hand appliquéd and quilted. 68 x 69 in. Collection of Joan Manda Swearingen Mueller.

that "we would scamper out of the room—but not until our too often disapproved stitching had been examined." A single square was perhaps all that a young and inexperienced student could handle, and it would have provided a manageable method for teaching sewing as well as for producing quilts for the needy on the mainland.

Whatever their original inspirations, by the 1870s Hawaiians had developed their own approach to quilt design, filling the entire top of their quilts with a single large appliqué that was usually patterned after island trees, plants, or flowers. The symmetrical and highly stylized designs were cut from a folded piece of solid-colored cotton cloth and appliquéd to a contrasting top, usually of solid white or cream. Early quilters could not be choosy about fabric. Although cotton was grown on Maui and Oahu in the nineteenth century, most cotton fabrics available in the islands were imported and therefore were relatively expensive. (Gins for processing cotton were apparently quite rare in Hawaii.) Quilters used bedsheets as the ground for their appliqué work and whatever they could find as backing material. Although many quilters used solid-colored fabric, a number of early quilts have appliqués cut from small printed calico. Common early color schemes for appliqués included red, deep blue, yellow, or orange on white. Pastel greens and purples were also sometimes used, and a few early quilters experimented with light-colored appliqués sewn onto dark backgrounds.

This basic approach is still followed by many quilters in the islands today. To make appliqué quilts, Hawaiians typically fold the piece of cloth from which the appliqué is to be cut in eighths. Usually the fabric is first folded in half vertically, the left side brought over to meet the right edge. The second fold is horizontal, again halving the fabric by bringing the top down to meet the bottom edge. The third and final fold creates a triangle by drawing the top right corner down to the lower left corner. The fabric is ironed after each fold to lay the seams as flat as possible. The quilter then pencils on the appliqué design, which, like the folded fabric, is exactly one-eighth the size of the quilt. Early quilters drew their designs freehand, directly on the cloth; paper and cloth patterns came into use late in the nineteenth century.

After tracing, the pattern is ready to be cut. All eight layers of the folded fabric are cut at the same time. (Some of today's quilters skip the folding by cutting around a full paper pattern.) Usually the border design is cut first and then the central design. After carefully unfolding the material to reveal the symmetrical cutwork design, the appliqué is placed on a solid-colored quilt top and, working from the center out to the edges and border, basted in place with long stitches. The basting holds the material in place while much finer and more closely spaced invisible hand appliqué stitching is applied to finish the job. When the needlework of the top is completed, batting is placed between the top and a backing fabric, which is usually a piece of solid-colored cloth that matches the background color of the top.

Both in technique and style, Hawaiian appliqué bears a striking resemblance to the cut paper work that was popular in the northeastern United States during the early decades of the nineteenth century. Many Pennsylvania Germans practiced *scherenschnitte*, a form of decorative folded paper cutting common in German-speaking areas of Europe. Similar cut paper designs were executed by New England schoolgirls, who crafted valentines, memorials, and pastoral pictures with their scissors. Although no documentary evidence has been found to confirm the theory, paper cutting may well have been introduced to Hawaii by missionaries who were familiar with it. Since cut paper pictures were made to be framed and hung or were bestowed as intimate gifts, they were obviously much smaller than Hawaiian appliqué designs. Both, however, were produced in exactly the same manner, by cutting multiple layers of folded material to produce a symmetrical design. And, like the appliqués, the designs of cut paper pieces were most often based on floral forms. It seems possible, perhaps even likely, that Hawaiian women saw and admired intricate and delicate cut paper work done by missionaries and applied the technique to their quiltmaking.

The use of cutout snowflakelike patterns as design elements in quilts probably was not a purely Hawaiian adaptation. In fact, Hawaiians may have had American-made examples to observe and copy. One home missionary society presentation quilt made in 1847 as a going-away present for a minister departing to Hawaii is made up of many small squares, each of which holds a cut paper pattern. Another existing album quilt, in the collection of the Honolulu Academy of Arts but, unfortunately, lacking any provenance, is made up of many small scherenschnitte squares, each looking very much like a miniature Hawaiian appliqué. It is perhaps no coincidence that the mainland American quilts that most closely resemble Hawaiian appliqué are of Pennsylvania German origin and were sometimes laid out with the help of the scherenschnitte design patterns. These quilts, especially those that use the plumelike Princess Feather pattern, either consist of a single large central medallion appliqué

that resembles Hawaiian technique or repeat the same floral design in four large blocks of equal size. Based on this sort of visual evidence, quilt researcher Joyce Gross has theorized that the first Hawaiian appliqué quilts may coincide with the founding of Hawaiian schools by Pennsylvania missionaries in the 1860s.

Although most of today's quilters stuff their quilts with polyester, early Hawaiians used a variety of natural materials for batting. Unprocessed wool and cotton commonly used by mainland American quilters was not always easy to come by in Hawaii, so other readily available materials were sometimes employed, including old blankets and the silky, hairlike "wool" that covers young, furled fronds of the hapu'u pulu tree fern. After the batting was in place, the three layers were ready to be sewn together with quilting stitches. The missionaries taught early island quilters the linear styles that were basic to their own sewing, but may also have passed on more decorative stitching patterns. Shells, for example, were a common stitching motif in early American quilts and became popular as well in the islands, perhaps as a result of contact with missionaries or missionary-made quilts. Of course, the abundance of shells in the environment no doubt also inspired their use by Hawaiian quilters. Other quilting patterns do seem to have been derived directly from Hawaiian sources. One of the most appealing of these is the turtle's back, in which mirrored image sets of progressively larger half ovals increase in size from a center line to recreate the shape of a sea turtle's back shell. The stitched turtleback motifs are usually set at 45-degree angles, like the petals of a flower, in mirrored groups of four, and are repeated over and over to cover the quilt.

The most common type of Hawaiian quilt stitching is contour or echo quilting, which repeats the inside and outside edges of the appliquéd design in tight waves that ripple outward to fill the entire surface of the quilt. The echoing parallel lines of quilting are typically spaced a finger's breadth apart to create a slightly raised, three-dimensional surface that provides a subtle visual and textural complement to the appliquéd design. One of the unique and defining elements of the Hawaiian appliqué quilt results from this method: the design can be felt as well as seen on

Scherenschnitte Quilt. Artist unknown. 1860–70. Honolulu Academy of Arts, Honolulu.
Plain woven, printed cotton, hand appliqué, hand quilting. Gift of Mrs. Herman Von Holt, 1949.

both sides of the quilt, the pattern on the otherwise undecorated back echoing and quietly repeating that on the front. It is not clear exactly how and when contour quilting originated but, like Hawaiian appliqué itself, contour quilting is seen on most of the earliest surviving island quilts, and it therefore seems reasonable that the concepts of contour quilting and folded appliqué arose simultaneously in the imaginations of early quiltmakers. Successful contour quilting is meticulous and time-consuming work that requires great patience and skill. A single contour-stitched quilt may contain over 200,000 hand stitches and take two or more years to complete, although many accomplished quiltmakers can complete a full-size quilt in three to six months.

Like North American Indians and other native and so-called primitive peoples around the world, early Hawaiians saw themselves as part of the natural world and believed that all of nature was infused with spirituality. Plants, animals, humans, mountains, tides, winds, storms, and volcanoes were all seen as sentient, interconnected parts of one vast whole, all related and each mutually dependent on the other for life and meaning, no one thing more or less important than another. The islands were viewed as a sacred ground which sustained all living things, and the land and its plants and animals were accorded respect, reverence, and care in return.

This intimate personal and spiritual relationship with the natural world, totally foreign to the Western Christian world view that the missionaries brought to the islands, lies at the heart of the Hawaiian quilt and is the key to understanding its subtle and often deeply hidden symbolic meanings. Unlike the missionaries, Hawaiians did not see themselves as above and separate from the natural world. They lacked the sense of "otherness" that in Western culture has allowed men to place themselves apart from nature as observers, scientists, landowners, exploiters, and developers. The Hawaiians' relationship with the natural world was a religious one, and their quilts were

extensions of this world view. The quilts were, therefore, not merely images of the natural world such as those found in a Western landscape or still-life painting but, rather, symbols of its spirit. Many nineteenth-century American quilters included floral or animal images in their appliqué quilts and, in the hands of a skillful seamstress, some of these representations could be quite realistic. Hawaiian quilters, in contrast, do not intend or attempt to depict nature realistically. Instead they create designs that recall natural forms and, in so doing, embody and elicit their inherent spirituality. By avoiding realism, the abstract appliqué patterns of Hawaiian quilts allow the viewer to see the real plant or animal form in his mind's eye and connect his own understanding with (and through) the image before him. In his book *The Unknown Craftsman: A Japanese Insight into Beauty*, Soetsu Yanagi explains this symbolic approach to nature, which applies to the works of native peoples worldwide: "There are many ways of seeing, but the truest and best is with the intuition, for it takes in the whole, whereas the intellect only takes in a part . . . Pattern is not realistic depiction . . . It is a product of the imagination . . . The pattern is a symbol of the plant, not the plant itself . . . A pattern is a picture of the essence of an object, an object's very life; its beauty is of that life . . . From the [plant] to the pattern there is a transformation, as from chrysalis to butterfly, taking life with it into a new form . . . Why should pattern be so beautiful? Because it provides unlimited scope for the imagination. Pattern does not explain; it leaves things to the viewer; its beauty is determined by [the] freedom it gives to the viewer's imagination."

Hawaiians also saw quilts as literal embodiments of their makers' spirits. Some quiltmakers, afraid that their spirits might be forced to wander after death, wanted to be sure their quilts were destroyed when they died or were buried with them. Hawaiian quilts were almost invariably made as gifts for family members or close friends. Quiltmaking was, above all else, an act of love. The quiltmaker concentrated on loving

thoughts of the recipient—her child, grandchild, husband, or neighbor—as she worked. Patterns and pattern names often carried private meanings known only to the quiltmaker, some of them too personal to be shared even with the receiver of the gift.

Missionaries were scarcely the only outside influences on the people of Hawaii, nor were they the earliest. Explorers, whalers, fur traders, and merchants from such disparate lands as Britain, France, Spain, Russia, and New England also found their way to the newly discovered islands in the late eighteenth and early nineteenth centuries, bringing shiploads of goods which could be traded and leaving the indelible marks of their own cultures, attitudes, and actions on the natives.

Hawaiians were fascinated by all of their visitors, observed them closely, and often imitated the new ways of life. Several early accounts indicate that at least some Hawaiians were familiar with Western sewing and clothing years before the first missionaries arrived. Archibald Campbell, a Scotsman who came to Hawaii aboard a Russian ship in 1809 and lived in the islands for two years, wrote of the Hawaiians, "It is astonishing how soon they acquire the useful arts from their visitors. Many of the natives are employed as carpenters, coopers, blacksmiths, and tailors, and do their work as perfectly as Europeans." And, writing in 1819, Louis de Freycinet, captain of the French ship *Uranie,* observed that "some of the chiefs have adopted the European type of clothing either completely or in part. . . . The same is true of women

Front of House. Hannah Kahilikolo and her grandchildren. 1930s. Kauai Museum.

living with whites on Wahou." Oriental influences were also present. Between 1800 and 1820, a booming trade in Hawaiian grown sandalwood brought an abundance of Chinese silks, cottons, and costumes to Hawaii. Scores of Russian ships transported the goods to and from China. A missionary descendant wrote that "Honolulu in 1820 had everything to sell that you could have found in the crossroad store at Brookfield or Cornwall or on the waterfront at Boston."

For the most part the Hawaiians welcomed foreigners and were quick to adopt new ways. But not all newcomers came with positive intent. During the middle decades of the nineteenth century, for example, at the same time the missionaries were establishing their presence on the islands, Hawaii was a center for the whaling industry. Pacific whaleships converged on Maui and Oahu twice a year, where they outfitted for the coming season of hunting. In March they readied for their summer in the Arctic hunting the bowhead whale and in November prepared for a winter of sperm whale hunting in the South Pacific. By the 1840s, over four hundred whaleships were stopping over in the islands each year; in the peak year of 1846 almost six hundred were in residence. These stopovers, which included all the pleasures of the flesh, were eagerly anticipated by the whalers. As one traditional whaleman's shanty rather discreetly put it:

> *Once more we're blown by the northern gales,*
> *And bounding o'er the main;*
> *And the green hills of them tropical isles*
> *We soon shall see again.*
> *Oh, it's many a day we toiled away*
> *In that cold Kamchatka Sea,*
> *And we'll think of that as we laugh and chat*
> *With the girls of old Maui.*

Clearly, the missionaries had their work cut out for them. In his *Maritime History of Massachusetts*, historian Samuel Eliot Morrison observed that the "missionaries arrived in the nick of time partially to offset the demoralization introduced by Boston traders and Nantucket whalers." Writing in *Roughing It*, Mark Twain, who visited the islands in 1866, offered a more immediate and considerably less charitable view: "The natives of the islands number only about 50,000 and the whites about 1,000, chiefly Americans. According to Capt. Cook, the natives numbered 400,000 less than a hundred years ago, but the traders brought labor and fancy diseases—in other words, long, deliberate, infallible destruction; and the missionaries brought the means of grace and got them ready. So the two forces are working along harmoniously, and anybody who knows anything about figures can tell you exactly when the last Kanaka will be in Abraham's bosom and his islands in the hands of the whites. It is the same as calculating an eclipse."

Although the missionaries, unlike the traders and whalemen, came to do what they considered holy work, Twain's insightful record points out that basically they were all representatives of the same foreign culture and that their relationship to each other was mutually dependent in many ways. More than a few Yankee captains were deeply religious men who helped support the missionaries' efforts. The missionaries in turn depended on the traders and whalers for supplies, mail, news from home, and transportation to and from the islands. Some Hawaiian women willingly accompanied captains on their voyages, and many Hawaiian men became whalers and seamen, providing much needed help on the often undermanned ships. Scores of these young Hawaiians were brought back to New York and New England in the first two decades of the nineteenth century, where they were often unable to make their own way. Early in the century, a "Foreign Mission School for the Sons of Unevangelized Barbarians" was formed in Cornwall, Connecticut, to minister to these displaced and often destitute young Hawaiians. The school publicized the islands' desperate need for salvation and became the direct forerunner of the overseas missionary effort that began in 1820. Indeed, four

Hawaiian boys from the school accompanied the first group of missionaries back to the islands, acting as interpreters and helping to promote the new religion among their people.

The American missionaries came to the islands with an ambitious agenda. "Your mission," read their authorizing document, "is a mission of mercy, and your work is to be wholly a labor of love . . . You are to aim at nothing short of covering those islands with fruitful fields and pleasant dwellings, and schools and churches; of raising the whole people to an elevated state of Christian civilization . . . it is an arduous enterprise, a great and difficult work. To obtain an adequate knowledge of the language of the people, to make them acquainted with letters; to give them the Bible with skill to read it; to turn them from their barbarous courses and habits; to introduce, and get into extended operation and influence among them, the arts and institutions and usages of civilized life and society . . . must be the work of an invincible and indefectible (*sic*) spirit of benevolence."

The influx of Western influences, exemplified in the missionaries' righteous agenda, brought sweeping and often profoundly unsettling change to Hawaii over the course of the nineteenth century. In a little over one hundred years, Hawaii was changed from an isolated native society to a Western colonial democracy dominated by the United States, which annexed the islands in 1898. When Europeans first came to Hawaii, they found a hierarchical society ruled by all-powerful chiefs. At the time of Cook's arrival, the islands were made up of four separate kingdoms, which were often at war with each other. The islands were first united into a single kingdom by the great chief Kamehameha I, who saw the coming of the Europeans as both a threat that demanded a strong unified government and an opportunity to gain personal political power. Starting from his inherited base of partial rule of the island of Hawaii, Kamehameha I, who was a brilliant warrior and a skillful politician, proceeded to conquer and assimilate the other islands one by one, gaining

control of all but Kauai by 1795. (Kauai held out until 1810, when the patient but persistent Kamehameha finally succeeded in bringing it under his rule.) He became the first king of the Hawaiian Islands, establishing a line of monarchs that combined Hawaiian and European traditions and ruled the islands until the forced abdication of Queen Lili'uokalani in 1893.

Throughout the nineteenth century Hawaii absorbed foreigners and foreign influences at a prodigious rate as European and American powers vied for political and economic control of the islands. Foreign investment and interests changed the islands' economy and racial makeup permanently. The developers soon demanded more workers than the islands could supply and brought many new people to Hawaii. Over 45,000 Chinese contract laborers were transported to Hawaii in the 1850s to work on the islands' booming sugar plantations. Many stayed and became part of Hawaii's changing racial mix. They were followed in the 1880s by scores of Japanese and Portuguese immigrants and, in the twentieth century, by over 125,000 Filipino workers. Koreans, Spaniards, Puerto Ricans, Russians, and people of many other ethnic backgrounds have joined the islands' remarkably tolerant international population over the years. Intermarriages have been frequent, and today, while 20 percent of islanders claim Hawaiian blood, less than one percent of the population is of pure Hawaiian ancestry.

Education also brought enormous changes. The strong example set by the missionary schools took quick and firm root in Hawaiian soil, and by 1840 schooling had became compulsory for all Hawaiians under the age of fourteen. Literacy became virtually universal. Using a bare bones alphabet of just seven consonants and five vowels, the missionaries created a written Hawaiian language and taught the islanders how to write it down. In return, a number of Hawaiian words—*aloha, luau, hula, muumuu, lei*—have entered the English language, which is now spoken by 99 percent of the Hawaiian population.

Hawaii's natural world was also affected dramatically by foreign influences. Much of Hawaii's native flora and fauna is now threatened or endangered by the encroachments of human development and by the influx of species brought to the islands from other parts of the world by man, either by intention or accident. These processes, of course, began as soon as humans set foot on the islands. The several species of large flightless birds that had evolved in Hawaii were no match for early Polynesian hunters, and all were extinct within years of contact. Some of the pigs brought by the first Polynesian settlers became feral; today, an estimated 100,000 of their progeny continue to wreak havoc with the landscape, rooting up native plants with their snouts and sowing alien species in their droppings. Disease-bearing rats also probably came with the first voyagers, and malarial mosquitoes arrived aboard American and European ships. Man's introduction of hundreds of other non-native plants and animals has challenged the islands' indigenous species and threatens their delicately balanced ecosystems.

Although traditional Hawaiian culture has also been diluted and even sometimes marginalized by the continuing barrage of foreign ideas and influences, traditional quiltmaking is alive and well in Hawaii. Today's Hawaiians are proud of their heritage, and an increasing number of tourists also now seek a deeper understanding of the islands' unique history and traditions. Along with such distinctive traditional Hawaiian arts as hula, chants, and slack key guitar music, quiltmaking has been revived in recent years by old and new practitioners and explored by art and cultural historians. All of the major museums in the islands include historic quilts in their collections, and quilt exhibitions are mounted regularly. Classes are taught throughout the islands by master quiltmakers, and many new quilters are encouraged to try their skills each year. While most quilters are content to copy the many beautiful traditional designs or create new floral patterns, a handful of adventurous quiltmakers including Elizabeth Akana, Sharon Balai,

Helen Friend, and Stan Yates are expanding the boundaries of the art form, creating expressive new designs and experimenting with such nontraditional concepts as double-sided quilts, mirror image patterns, and reverse appliqué.

This study presents a selection of forty-eight Hawaiian quilts, chosen from a variety of museum and private collections, which span the entire history of the art form, from early experiments to the work of contemporary masters. Each of these remarkable quilts is a masterpiece in cloth, a work executed with extraordinary skill which illuminates part of the Hawaiian tradition. Although Hawaiians are best known for their stunning floral appliqués, other island forms deserve wider recognition. In addition to a number of floral masterpieces, the book therefore also offers outstanding examples of bark cloth bedcovers, delicate embroidered pieces, and Hawaiian flag quilts and other patriotic designs, as well as a distinctive pieced Log Cabin and a historic crazy quilt made by Lili'uokalani, the last monarch of the islands. Whether notable for its design, craftsmanship, innovation, provenance, or historical associations, each quilt included in this book embodies the spirit of Hawaiian quilting by paying loving tribute to the islands.

Whether stitched by a nineteenth-century native or one of today's fabric artists, all Hawaiian quilts require special care. Hawaii's moist tropical climate has always been hard on quilts, which are susceptible to mildew and rot in the warm, damp air and are also eaten by some island insects. Exposure to bright sunlight also damages fabric. Ultraviolet light can fade colors drastically, ultimately destroying the contrast between appliqué and background. Thousands of Hawaiian quilts have undoubtedly fallen prey to the climate, which unfortunately continues to threaten historic quilts in both private and museum collections. In earlier days, quilts were simply not expected to last too long, and their obsolescence was carefully planned. When a quilt began to show the effects of the environment, a copy was made to insure that its design would survive from generation to generation. In recent years, advancements in climate control and modern conservation techniques have helped save some historic quilts, although lack of knowledge and inadequate storage conditions still threaten the islands' heritage. Museums in the islands are increasingly diligent, carefully monitoring quilts in storage and on exhibit for any signs of trouble and cleaning and/or fumigating quilts that have been exposed to pests or spores.

The Hawaiian Quilt Research Project, founded in 1990 by Elizabeth Akana and documentary filmmaker Elaine Zinn, has unearthed hundreds of previously unknown quilts and done much to raise public consciousness of the importance of the art form as an element of traditional Hawaiian identity and culture. Volunteers working for the research project have held quilt days on the six major islands and expect to continue the search for quilts dating before 1960 through 1997. The project encourages quilt owners to bring heirloom quilts out to be

photographed, measured, and recorded for posterity. Thus far over eight hundred quilts and over six hundred patterns in museum and private collections have been examined and documented by the project. Because patterns are such an important part of the Hawaiian tradition, the project has made a special effort to record them, first photographing the paper or cloth patterns and then scanning the photos into a computer database. The project researcher can then manipulate the one-eighth pattern into a complete quilt design on screen. A number of previously unidentified or misidentified quilts have already been reunited with their correct pattern names through the database.

Both as concept and reality, Hawaii continues to fascinate people around the world. Mark Twain spoke for many visitors to Hawaii when he wrote, "No alien land in all the world has any deep strong charm for me but that one, no other land could so longingly and so beseechingly haunt me, sleeping and waking, through half a lifetime, as that one has done. Other things leave me, but it abides; other things change, but it remains the same. For me its balmy airs are always blowing, its summer seas flashing in the sun; the pulsing of its surfbeat is in my ear; I can see its garlanded crags, its leaping cascades, its plumy palms drowsing by the shore, its remote summits floating like islands above the cloud rack; I can feel its woodland solitudes, I can hear the plash of its brooks; in my nostrils still lives the breath of flowers that perished twenty years ago." All the qualities that so haunted Twain are present in Hawaii's quilts. They are ambassadors of the islands, created out of love for these unique lands and between the people who live on them. Intended as personal gifts, they are now gifts to us all, reminding us of the fragile and almost incomprehensible beauty of America's most exotic state and inviting us to understand how we might still live in harmony with the natural world. Their message is subtle but profound, and it has never been more timely.

Elizabeth Akana and Gussie Bento examining a quilt for the Hawaiian Quilt Research Project.

HAWAIIAN QUILT MASTERPIECES

The Davies Family Quilt

Artist unknown · 1874

This early and unusual quilt was made to celebrate the sixth birthday of Clive Davies, the eldest son of Theophilus H. Davies, at the time the most prominent English businessman in the islands. At the quilt's center is the British coat of arms, flanked by a stout crowned British lion and a chained unicorn and topped by a substantial crown. The four panels of the coat of arms include an Irish harp, a representation of the Scottish lion, and two panels of three horses. A large Maltese cross is appliquéd on either side of the central crown, while the name "Davies" and the boy's anniversary date of "September 28, 1874" appear beneath the coat of arms. A symmetrical motif of four leaves around a circle is repeated in each corner of the quilt, and a wreath of crossed laurel branches at top center balances the lettering below the coat of arms. The two floral motifs add a distinctly Hawaiian flavor to the otherwise properly British emphasis of the design elements. The letters "NA," probably the initials of the presumably Hawaiian quiltmaker, are stitched in red at the lower front corner.

Theophilus Harris Davies was a Honolulu-based merchant and financier whose Theo. H. Davies and Company, Limited, remains one of the major landholders and business conglomerates in the islands. The firm, founded in 1845 by another Englishman, was bought by Davies in the 1850s. Under his guidance, it expanded into the sugar business and became one of the so-called Big Five, the small group of wholly foreign-owned corporations that developed, controlled, and managed much of Hawaii's land and commercial activity in the second half of the nineteenth century. In addition to his varied business interests, Davies also served as British vice-consul of Hawaii for a time. He moved back to Britain in 1890, where he acted as guardian of Princess Ka'iulani during her years of education in England. In 1892 he traveled to Washington with Ka'iulani, where he unsuccessfully tried to persuade lawmakers to support a regency with his young ward replacing the troublesome (and less easily controlled) Queen Lili'uokalani, whose government fell to the Americans the following year.

Hawaiian Islands. Cottons, hand appliquéd and quilted. 93 1/2 x 66 in. Collection of Geoffrey Davies and family, made for Theophilus Clive Davies, son of Theophilus H. Davies, for his sixth birthday.

Lei O Ka'ahumanu

Artist unknown · c. 1880

This late nineteenth-century quilt, given to the owner's family in 1959 by a fisherman friend, is probably typical of the first ventures at appliqué design attempted by Hawaiians. It consists only of a central folded cutout pattern, without border embellishments. A single cutout floral form set at right angles and repeated four times makes up the central design. The powerful and well-conceived pattern fills the quilt's square top nicely, leaving a pleasingly complex balance of positive and negative space that keeps the eye moving over the varied symmetrical shapes.

Several names have been attached to this popular design over the years, obscuring its true identity and origin. A paper pattern for the design in the Hannah Ku'umililani Cummings Baker collection at the Bishop Museum is incorrectly identified as Mamo Lei, an error that apparently first appeared in the early Hawaiian quilt researcher Stella Jones's 1930 book. Jones included a photo of another quilt of this design which was mistakenly identified as Mamo Lei. Even though the error was corrected by an errata

sheet issued with the book, it was too late; more people read the photo caption than the correction, and the name has been associated with the design ever since. The incorrect name Acorn has also become attached to the design, again apparently through a corrected mistake in the Jones book. Another pattern for the design, in the collection of the Waianae Library in Honolulu, gives the name as Lei O Ka'ahumanu, which may or may not be historically correct. It is to be hoped that further research will ultimately uncover other quilts or patterns that reveal some definitive information about this marvelous design's early history.

Ka'ahumanu was one of the twenty-one wives of King Kamehameha I, the founder of the Hawaiian kingdom and monarchy. Ka'ahumanu, who was the king's favorite wife, outlived her husband and became co-ruler of the kingdom after his death in 1819. She claimed that she was the voice of the dead king's will, and she wielded enormous indirect power both because of her connection with him and her own formidable personality.

Hawaiian Islands. Cottons, hand appliquéd and quilted. 82 ¾ x 82 ¾ n. Collection of Ursula D. J. Yee.

Central Plumed Star

Artist unknown · c. 1880

This quilt's central design bears a striking resemblance to the traditional Princess Feather pattern, a widely distributed American design that was particularly popular among mid-nineteenth-century Pennsylvania German quiltmakers. Although many mainland quiltmakers used the Princess Feather motif only as an element (a feather medallion placed at the center of the quilt, or repeated motifs in different blocks), it was also one of the few American patterns that was made into a single large appliqué, a technique similar to that later used by Hawaiian quiltmakers.

Pennsylvania German missionaries came to Hawaii in the 1860s, and the fact that this quilt is dated sometime after is strong evidence that the Princess Feather design of identically shaped lacy feathers set around a central star shape may have been seen and imitated by Hawaiian quiltmakers. Although no documentary evidence exists, many quilt historians believe that Hawaiians learned cutout techniques derived from the Pennsylvania German traditional cut paper art

called *scherenschnitte*. Some Pennsylvania German quilters are known to have applied scherenschnitte techniques to quilt design, cutting intricate paper patterns for individual blocks of album quilts. Indeed, one such album quilt is known to have been made as a gift for a missionary on his way to Hawaii. Its blocks are a mixture of such well-known patterns as Mariner's Compass and Nine-Patch, with the addition of cut paper snowflakes that look like miniature Hawaiian appliqués. It seems reasonable to conclude that Hawaiian women saw and were influenced by such quilts and combined the ideas of the overall Princess Feather type appliqué and the cutout work of scherenschnitte to create their own approach to quilt design.

The floral motif that repeats in each of this remarkable quilt's four corners is unusually large, vying with the central motif for the viewer's attention. The "feathers" of the central motif are repeated in the corners as leaves and are the same size in both designs.

Hawaiian Islands. Cottons, hand appliquéd and quilted. 80 x 80 in.
The Shelburne Museum, Shelburne, Vermont. Gift of George Frelinghuysen.

Na Kalaunu Me Ka Lei Maile

[CROWNS AND MAILE LEI]

Artist unknown · c. 1880

Many Hawaiian quilts show evidence of damage from ultraviolet light, a component of ordinary sunlight which can bleach and otherwise alter colors and cause fabric to deteriorate. In addition to damage from light, Hawaiian quilts are also threatened by mildew and cloth-eating insects such as moths and beetles. Soiling and wear and tear from normal handling and use can also take a toll over the course of time. In the case of this 115-year-old quilt, the appliqué design, which was originally white, has become slightly discolored with a light greenish/yellow tinge. Also, small pieces of the appliqué have worn off, revealing tiny patches of the underlying red ground. Happily, however, the damage is relatively minor; the quilt is otherwise in very good condition, and proper storage will probably succeed in preserving it for future generations to enjoy and study.

This quilt's unusually structured pattern combines appliqué elements of one-, two- and three-fold complexity, resulting in designs which appear once, twice, or four times respectively. While Hawaiian quiltmakers created entire designs based on one, two, or, most commonly, three folds, they rarely combined approaches in a single quilt. In this stunning exception to the rule, the small design element at the center of the quilt is only symmetrical when divided in half vertically, and was thus conceived as a single fold. The same design is repeated in a larger size to the left and right of the center of the quilt; these elements are mirror images set vertically at right angles to the central design and thus represent a two-fold symmetry. The rest of the quilt's design, including the four crowns and leis in the central field and the vining border that surrounds them, is built on a more typical three-fold symmetry.

Hawaiian Islands. Cottons, hand appliquéd and quilted. 72 1/2 x 68 1/2 in. Daughters of Hawaii, Honolulu.

Log Cabin

Great-grandmother of Joseph Makini · c. 1880

The Log Cabin is probably the best known and most widely disseminated of all American pieced quilt designs. The first Log Cabin quilts were made around the time of the Civil War, and the pattern reached the height of its popularity in the last quarter of the nineteenth century. Log Cabins have been made by African-American and Amish quilters as well as thousands of other quiltmakers and have been worked in wool and silk as well as a wide variety of cottons. The overall pattern of a Log Cabin design is determined by the arrangement of colors, and the range of possibilities is inviting and seemingly endless. Little wonder Log Cabins continue to be a favorite among contemporary quilters.

The Log Cabin's broad popularity helps explain its appearance in this late nineteenth-century Hawaiian quilt. The quiltmaker has, however, adapted the Log Cabin by reworking its elements to create something radically different from the mainland examples she must have seen. A typical Log Cabin, or for that matter any pieced quilt, is made up of dozens of small blocks. By building the top of only sixteen very large pieced blocks, the maker of this quilt has adjusted the quilt's scale. Her choice and arrangement of colors are also distinctive. The close values of the lighter yellow and orange create a soft and relatively uniform background against which the strong contrasting strips of red and blue, some of the latter now faded to a gray-green, stand out. The placement of the darker colors in the two squares at bottom middle also confounds expectations by throwing the quilt's color rhythms out of symmetry, creating an active, unpredictable overall composition. Given the large size of the blocks, this bit of asymmetry heightens the quilt's visual interest by keeping the viewer's eye moving constantly across the composition.

Kauai. Cottons, hand pieced and quilted. 80 x 79 in. Honolulu Academy of Arts, Honolulu.

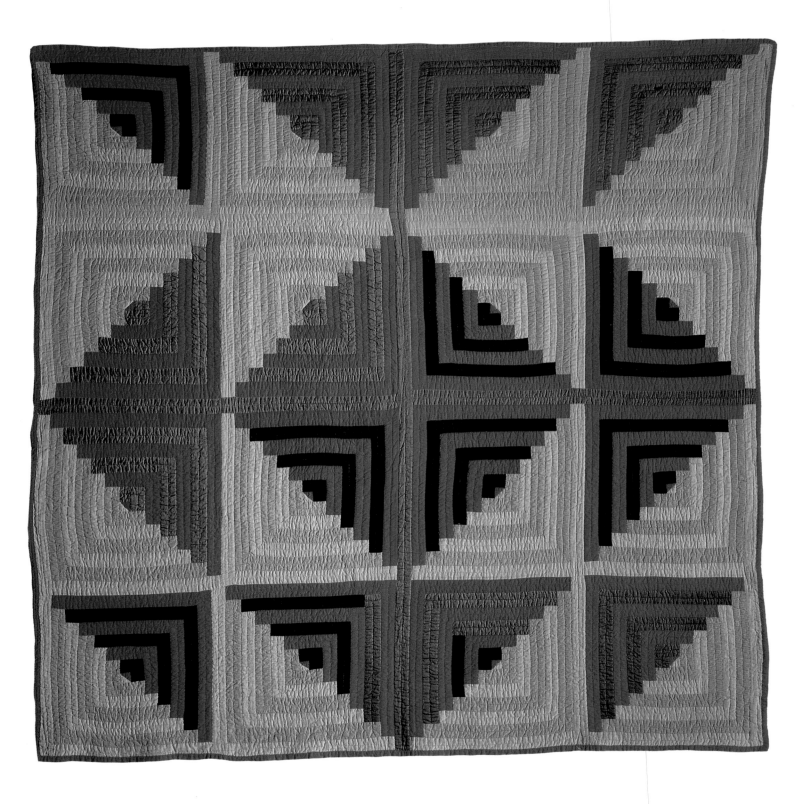

Unnamed Floral Pattern

Artist unknown · Before 1918

Before contact, Hawaiians made cloth called tapa from pounded sheets of bark from the paper mulberry tree. The designs that decorate this quilt and sheet of tapa bark cloth are clearly closely related, indicating that over the course of the nineteenth century Hawaiians adapted traditional approaches to decorating their bark cloth bedcovers to the new medium of quilting.

Hawaiians often decorated tapa cloth bedcovers, called *kapa moe,* with designs derived from native flora. *Kapa moe* were made of several sheets of tapa, which were either left their natural white or dyed a solid color and then sewn together with strands of bark thread. Like a multilayered quilt, only the top sheet of the *kapa moe* bedcover, which was almost always dyed, was decorated. A second, contrasting dye was used to stencil the designs, which were typically repeated symmetrical forms. This approach to design is similar to that of early Hawaiian quiltmakers, who cut large repeating floral designs from cotton cloth and appliquéd them onto sheets of solid-colored background cloth.

In adapting the printed tapa pattern to appliquéd cloth, the quilt designer reduced the size of the basic pattern and eliminated the single central image. In its place this artist created a far more complex design by closing the repeating forms of the tapa pattern into a circle; a border of closely related floral forms, set in a solid outer band, frames the central motif.

Although the name of this design is not known, it does resemble two other traditional patterns, called Dahlia and Champak Blossom, and may be related to either or both. A second quilt using this design is in the collection of the Mission Houses Museum in Honolulu; the quiltmaker turned the design in that example sideways on point, necessitating a minor change in the border to make it fit.

Above: Tapa Cloth. Artist unknown. Before 1914. Hawaiian Islands. Collected by Lewa Iokia.
Pounded paper mulberry bark, natural dyes. 63 x 55 ⅛ in. The Field Museum, Chicago, Illinois. Gift of Catherine Pope.
Right: Hawaiian Islands. Probably made for Mr. and Mrs. William Richards Castle.
Cottons, hand appliquéd and quilted. 84 ½ x 82 ½ in. The Field Museum, Chicago, Illinois.

Kuli Puʻu

[BENT KNEE]

Artist unknown · c. 1880–1910

Unlike the placid mood projected by most Hawaiian quilts, this unique and powerful design crackles with energy. The aptly suggestive pattern name is written on the quilt's back. The bold multi-colored zigzag design is visually reminiscent of the graphic Lightning Bolt pattern sometimes worked in bright colors by Mennonite quiltmakers in the American Midwest, but is actually closely related to the decorative pattern of the bark cloth *kapa moe* bedcover seen on this page.

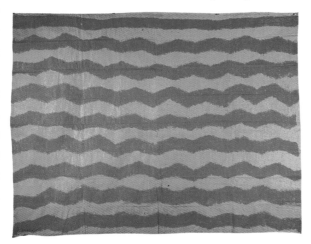

The quilt's rich red, white, and blue colors are similar to those used in many flag quilts and may be subtle reminders of the royal Hawaiian flag. Hand quilting echoes the zigzag lines of the design over most of the surface, while the quilt's edges are machine stitched. The thin dark blue outer band contains the explosive pattern, adding further tension to the design.

Although flag quilts combined piecing and appliqué in their designs, fully pieced Hawaiian quilts like this one are extremely rare. Only a handful of examples exist, and apparently few were made in the nineteenth century. Hawaiians undoubtedly saw American (and perhaps British) pieced quilts, but they did not follow those examples, preferring instead to find their own approach to designing and decorating quilts. And, once the Hawaiian appliqué tradition was well established, island quiltmakers rarely saw reason to look to American design traditions for inspiration or expression.

While American quilt patterns are usually linear and hard edged, Hawaiian patterns are full of gentle curves based on natural forms. The abstract geometric patterns typical of American quiltmaking undoubtedly seemed utterly foreign to Hawaiian quilters, whose flowing appliqué designs derived from their close relationship to the natural world and evoked a host of subtle symbolic meanings. The cultural and interpersonal continuity and symbolism they communicated were of particular importance to island quiltmakers.

Above: Kapa Moe. Artist unknown. 19th century. Hawaiian Islands. Pounded and threaded paper mulberry bark, natural dye. 69 ¼ x 85 ³⁄₁₆ in. The Field Museum, Chicago, Illinois. Collected by the maternal Hawaiian forebears of Mrs. L. Byron Nash between 1870 and 1910. Gift of Mrs. Nash.
Right: Kauai. Cottons, hand pieced, appliquéd, and quilted, with machine-stitched edging. 92 x 82 in. Honolulu Academy of Arts, Honolulu. Gift of Mrs. Charles M. Cooke.

Roses

Artist unknown · Late 19th/early 20th century

This quilt's flowers were probably intended to represent roses, which grew in abundance in the gardens at Queen Emma's elegant summer palace located in the hills above Honolulu. The palace is now maintained as a museum by the Daughters of Hawaii, an organization founded in 1903 by daughters of American missionaries "to perpetuate the memory and spirit of old Hawaii and to preserve the nomenclature and correct pronunciation of the Hawaiian language."

Queen Emma, born Emma Rooke, was the wife of Alexander Liholiho, King Kamehameha IV. The pair had been childhood sweethearts. Emma was the granddaughter of an Englishman named John Young, who had been a trusted advisor of King Kamehameha I in the early years of the century, and was also the great-granddaughter of Kamehameha I's brother. Both King Kamehameha IV and Queen Emma were well-educated aristocrats with sophisticated tastes and interests. They maintained close ties with Queen Victoria, who agreed to be godmother to their only child, and they brought much of the pomp and circumstance of the British royal tradition to the islands.

Emma was a leader of fashion and surrounded herself with a coterie of beautiful young women, who, like her, were of mixed Hawaiian and white blood. Her deeply religious husband translated *The Book of Common Prayer* into Hawaiian and brought a London clergyman to Honolulu to be the first Episcopal bishop of the city. The royal couple founded Queen's Hospital, the islands' first public hospital, as well as St. Andrew's Cathedral. Their happy and progressive reign was tragically short lived, however; their son Andrew died suddenly in 1862 at age four, and the heartbroken king died a year later. Emma, who lost a later bid to regain the throne, died in 1885.

Hawaiian Islands. Cottons, hand and machine pieced, hand appliquéd and quilted. 77 ½ x 77 ½ in.
Daughters of Hawaii, Queen Emma Summer Palace, Honolulu. Gift of Mr. and Mrs. Thomas Guard, Jr.

Na Kihapai Nani Lue'ole O Edena A Me Elenale

[THE BEAUTIFUL UNEQUALED GARDENS OF EDEN AND ELENALE]

Artist unknown · Late 19th/early 20th century

Although several men are active in Hawaiian quiltmaking today, this unique quilt is one of the few historic examples believed to have been made by a man. The original owner told officials at the Honolulu Academy of Arts that it had been made "by a great-great-granduncle of my husband and handed down to him by an uncle," a most uncommon lineage for any quilt.

The quilt's two pictorial sections juxtapose a scene out of Hawaiian legend with a central image of the Christian religion brought to Hawaii by American missionaries in the nineteenth century. The right side of the quilt depicts Adam and Eve in the Garden of Eden, while the left side presents Elenale and Leinaala, the mythical hero and heroine of a popular nineteenth-century Hawaiian romance. The story of Elenale and Leinaala was the first literary work ever published in Hawaiian, which was a strictly oral language until it was codified by the missionaries. In it the supernatural Elenale grew up in an eponymous

magic garden, which Hawaiians considered second only to Eden in its pristine beauty. Elenale fell in love with the earthly princess Leinaala and rescued her from a witch who held her captive. The quiltmaker apparently modeled his image of Leinaala after a photograph of the fashionable Queen Emma, and dressed the couple in royal garb.

Hawaii has long been considered a paradise on Earth by Westerners, often inviting comparison with the Biblical garden paradise of man's innocence. In *Roughing It,* Mark Twain, not known for his sentiment, wrote tenderly, "I have visited, a great many years ago, the [Hawaiian] Islands—that peaceful land, that beautiful land, that far off home of profound repose, and soft indolence, and dreamy solitude, where life is one long slumberless Sabbath, the climate one long delicious summer day, and the good that die experience no change, for they but fall asleep in one heaven and wake up in another."

Hawaiian Islands. Cottons, hand appliquéd and quilted. 86 x 98 in. (including fringe).
Honolulu Academy of Arts, Honolulu. Gift of Mrs. Charles M. Cooke.

Quilt for Queen Lili'uokalani

Artist unknown · c. 1893

Queen Lili'uokalani, the last monarch of the Hawaiian kingdom, reigned only from January 1891 to January 1893, when she was forced to relinquish control of the islands to a provisional government that favored the islands' annexation by the United States. Today, far removed from the turmoil that marked her brief reign, she is best remembered as the composer of Hawaii's most familiar song, the achingly beautiful "Aloha Oe."

Lili'uokalani was a complex and strong-minded woman whose deeply held beliefs about the prerogatives of the monarchy led inevitably to clashes with an island legislature controlled by foreign business interests. She came to power at a crucial moment. The sugar industry, which had become Hawaii's dominant income generator, was seriously depressed, and the islands' constitutional government was rocked by racial unrest, battling foreign interests, and the threat of insurrection by both natives or foreigners. Many parties believed that the situation could only be stabilized if the United States took control of the islands, annexing them as a territory and settling the question of sovereignty once and for all.

The queen seriously misjudged both her power and the complexity of the situation, and when she declared in January 1893 that she would soon proclaim a new constitution, the annexationists moved against her. American troops stationed on a ship in Honolulu harbor were called in to restore order by United States Minister John L. Stevens, who supported the aims of the annexationists. A provisional government was quickly established, martial law was declared, and the queen, outmaneuvered and unwilling to shed blood, surrendered her government, under protest, "to the superior force of the United States of America." Frustrated by diplomatic efforts to reinstate the monarchy, Lili'uokalani's stubborn and sometimes tactless actions during the next two years undoubtedly helped put the final nails in the monarchy's coffin.

Hawaiian Islands. Cottons, hand appliquéd and quilted. 98 x 96 in. Collection of Washington Place, Hawaii's Governor's Home.

Queen Liliʻuokalani's Crazy Quilt

Queen Liliʻuokalani and assistants · c. 1895

Late in 1894, almost two years after the Hawaiian monarchy had been overthrown, a group of royalists began planning a coup against the provisional government. They stockpiled contraband arms, even hiding some in the queen's flower gardens. Word of the plot leaked to the government, however, and early in January 1895 the conspirators were sought and eventually arrested. Liliʻuokalani was arrested on January 16 and confined to a special prison room within her former palace, now the seat of the provisional government. After a substantial cache of arms was discovered on the grounds of her home, the queen was put on trial for knowledge of treasonous acts. Although found guilty and sentenced to five years hard labor and a $5,000 fine, the sentence was not carried out: she was later pardoned and her full citizenship privileges were reinstated.

This quilt, a remarkable document of this tragic phase of Hawaiian history, bears the embroidered phrase: "Imprisoned at ʻIolani Palace. We began this quilt there." Also embroidered on the quilt are dates of the queen's birth, ascension to the throne, dethronement, arrest, and abdication, as well as the names of the queen's supporters and women who assisted in completing the quilt. Tiny pairs of crossed Hawaiian flags appear at each corner of the quilt's central square.

Crazy quilts, named for the "crazed" shattered glass appearance of their unevenly sized pieces and heavy, decorative embroidery stitches, were all the rage in late Victorian America. They were, however, rarely made by Hawaiians. While many mainland crazies were carefully assembled from silks bought especially for the project, queen Liliʻuokalani's quilt was crafted from scraps cut from dresses, ribbons, and other available fabrics. The quilt is composed of nine squares which are bordered by maroon fabric; each square is in effect a miniature crazy quilt. Three of the squares are simply pieced of plain colored fabric and covered with embroidered words, while the remaining squares carry many small pieces in typical crazy quilt style.

Honolulu, Oahu. Silks, hand pieced and embroidered. 98 ⅝ x 96 in. Friends of the ʻIolani Palace, Honolulu.

Crossed Flags Quilt

Artist unknown · Late 19th/early 20th century

The royal Hawaiian flag's design was a combination of the red, white, and blue stripes of the American flag and the Union Jack of the British flag. It consisted of alternating red, white, and blue stripes representing the major islands of Hawaii, with the Union Jack placed in the upper left corner. The Hawaiian flag first took its standard eight-stripe shape in 1845, when Kauai, which was previously a territory, officially became part of the kingdom.

The Hawaiian flag had great meaning for the people of the islands, and many quilts were made that incorporated representations of the flag into their designs. The great majority of flag quilts were created in response to the two events which signaled the end of Hawaii's brief period of political independence. First, after bringing the kingdom to the brink of open hostilities between natives and white landholders, the ambitious Queen Lili'uokalani was deposed in a coup in January 1893 and ultimately was forced to abdicate her throne. The second and final blow came in 1898, when the islands were annexed by the United States, never more to hold independent status or to be ruled by a monarchy. The islands remained American territories until they were granted statehood in 1959.

Flag quilts typically included pieced representations of four elongated Hawaiian flags. The pieced flags were set at right angles to each other around an appliquéd central medallion, which usually represented the Hawaiian coat of arms. This unusual quilt breaks the standard format of the flag quilt by setting four small pairs of Hawaiian flags around a central coat of arms. The entire surface of the quilt is covered with carefully quilted diamonds, which are particularly striking against the considerable white space left by the open design.

Hawaiian Islands. Cottons, hand pieced, appliquéd, and quilted. 90 1/2 x 84 1/2 in.
Honolulu Academy of Arts, Honolulu. Gift of Mrs. Levi Lawrence.

Ku'u Hae Aloha

[MY BELOVED FLAG]

Artist unknown · Early 20th century

Flag quilts were made to honor and memorialize the short-lived Hawaiian kingdom and its brief period of international independence, which lasted slightly less than one hundred years. Royal Hawaiian flag quilts are known collectively by the name *Ku'u Hae Aloha,* an inscription often found on the quilts that means "my beloved flag" or "lost beloved flag." The quilts also pay homage to the kingdom's kings and queens, who were revered by the common people of the islands. Because of Hawaiians' high regard for the old kingdom, flag quilts were treasured above all others by their owners, who kept their existence a secret to all but family members and their most intimate and trusted friends. To this day, flag quilts remain prized and hidden treasures by many families in the islands.

This complex flag quilt is a superior example of the form in its most recognizable and fully mature state, probably made after the islands were annexed by the United States in 1898. Four Hawaiian flags are pieced around a central motif of Hawaiian royal symbols. The eight stars undoubtedly stand for the eight major islands of the Hawaiian chain, as do the eight stripes on each of the flags. The Hawaiian seal did not include stars until after Queen Lili'uokalani was deposed in 1893, so the quilt must have been made after that event. Apart from the stars, which are an unusual touch, the center field includes most of the elements commonly found in the flag quilt: the words *"Ku'u Hae Aloha,"* large and small royal crowns, an ermine cape, and a representation of the Hawaiian shield. The design is completed at the bottom by a pair of branches ending in single flowers, perhaps meant to represent roses. The center of the quilt is stitched with patterns that echo the various design elements, while the flags are quilted in straight lines that repeat their stripes.

Hawaiian Islands. Cottons, hand pieced, appliquéd, and quilted. 74 1/2 x 79 in.
Honolulu Academy of Arts, Honolulu. Gift of Mrs. Helmuth W. Hormann.

Na Kalaunu, Me Ka Lei

[CROWN AND WREATH]

Artist unknown · c. 1900

This simple design enlarges the single royal crown found on the 1845 Hawaiian coat of arms into a bold central motif and surrounds the crown with a laurel wreath. The crown and wreath are framed by an equally uncomplicated outside floral border.

Unlike most Hawaiian appliqués, this quilt's design was apparently cut after only one fold of the cloth, so that it divides into left/right mirror images on either side of the central vertical line. Typically, Hawaiian appliqués are cut after three folds to produce an interlocking, repeating symmetrical design that is based on a one-eighth section of the square. The choice of a single crown as the central design element for this quilt made such multidirectional symmetry impossible; a three-fold approach would have probably required incorporating four smaller crowns into the overall design. This quiltmaker clearly wanted to emphasize the crown rather than reduce it to an element in a complex design scheme and chose a simpler and more direct approach to achieve that end.

Hawaiian monarchs were strongly influenced by the royal traditions of Great Britain, which they combined with their own ancient ceremonies and trappings. The result, especially in the first half of the nineteenth century, was a unique and sometimes curious mix of European and Polynesian pomp with Christian and polytheistic circumstance. Feather capes, for instance, were symbols of power first worn by the early rulers of the islands. Island kings employed royal bird catchers who traveled deep into the upland rain forests to capture rare honeycreepers, sometimes taking just a few select feathers from hundreds or even thousands of birds to make up a single cape. The feather cape remained an important symbol of royal power well into the nineteenth century; instead of being replaced by such European traditions as crowns and scepters, it was used alongside these newly adopted British symbols. Both crown and feather cape are known to have been worn by mid-century Hawaiian kings.

Hawaiian Islands. Cottons, hand appliquéd and quilted. 78 ¼ x 77 ¼ in. Daughters of Hawaii, Honolulu.

Embroidered Plumes

Amy Hobbs Maihikoa · c. 1904

Amy Hobbs Maihikoa made this delicate embroidered quilt as a wedding present for her daughter. Sixteen pairs of embroidered plumes set in a variety of orientations decorate the quilt, which is also covered with intricate hand quilt stitching.

Women have decorated quilt tops with embroidery since the late 1700s. Early British and American quilters often added embroidered flowers or other designs to central medallion quilts, and many unquilted summer bedspreads were decorated with elaborate embroidery only. Blocks for album quilts, made by groups of women as gifts or as fundraising efforts, were often signed with embroidery stitches. During the Victorian era, embroidery was a major element of most crazy quilts; a wide variety of decorative embroidery stitches were used to join the unevenly shaped and sized pieces that typically made up the quilts, and embroidered signatures and other notations were often added.

Embroidered red-on-white quilts were quite popular in the late nineteenth and early twentieth centuries in both the United States and Hawaii. The embroidered designs on these quilts were usually simple and often consisted of one or sometimes two repeated forms. For less creative or skilled quilters, iron-on transfers and even sheets of muslin with prestamped patterns were available in stores or through the mail; both were widely used by young girls as needlework study pieces.

Unlike quilting, which joins all three layers of the quilt and is visible on both the top and back, thereby serving a structural function and adding a textural quality, embroidery only pierces the top layer and is purely decorative. As seen in this example, quilting often uses thread the same color as the ground so that the quilting pattern can only be detected on close inspection, while embroidery is almost always worked in a contrasting color.

Kauai. Cotton, hand embroidered and quilted. 79 x 77 ½ in. Mission Houses Museum, Honolulu. Gift of Doris DeRego, 1993.

Fan and Feather Plume

Artist unknown · Early 20th century

The Fan and Feather Plume is a traditional pattern often worked by island quilters. Because a pair of warrior chiefs holding feather plume standards were depicted on the royal Hawaiian coat of arms, this popular design motif, like a flag quilt, held sentimental meaning for island quiltmakers. The stylized fans and plumes and stark red-on-white color scheme make this a powerful graphic design. On this example, the quiltmaker has framed the traditional pattern with a floral border.

A missionary's account of a parade, organized by King Liholiho in 1823 on the anniversary of the death of King Kamehameha I, describes the pageant and splendor of early Hawaiian royalty that this quilt evokes: "The *car of state* consisted of an elegantly modeled *whale boat,* fastened firmly to a platform or frame of light spars, thirty feet long by twelve wide; and borne on the heads or shoulders of seventy men . . . [wearing] splendid scarlet and yellow feather cloaks and helmets . . . The only dress of the queen was a scarlet silk pau, or silk petticoat, and a coronet of feathers. She was seated in the middle of the boat and screened from the sun by an immense Chinese umbrella of scarlet damask, richly ornamented with gilding, fringe, and tassels, and supported by a chief standing behind her in a scarlet malo or girdle, and feather helmet. On one quarter of the boat stood Kalanimoku, the prime minister; and on the other, Naihe, the national orator; both also in malos of scarlet silk and helmets of feathers, and each bearing a kahili or feathered staff of state, near thirty feet in height. The upper part of these kahili were of scarlet feathers, so ingeniously and beautifully arranged . . . as to form cylinders fifteen or eighteen inches in diameter and twelve or fourteen feet long; the lower parts or handles were covered with alternate rings of tortoise shell and ivory, of the neatest workmanship and highest polish."

Hawaiian Islands. Cottons, hand appliquéd and quilted. 83 x 75 in.
American Museum in Britain, Claverton Manor, Bath, United Kingdom.

Na Kalaunu

[CROWNS]

Artist unknown · Early 20th century

This quilt's unusual color scheme replaces the typical high contrast of a dark appliqué on a light ground that is found in most Hawaiian quilt designs with two rarely used colors of almost equal value and intensity. Furthermore, the two colors are not really harmonious, so their juxtaposition creates a visual tension not often found in the typically restful color combinations chosen by most Hawaiian quiltmakers. The strong mustardy orange-yellow color of the ground advances in the viewer's eye and thus directly competes for attention with the purple appliqué designs.

The impact of the appliqué designs is also softened somewhat by their number and relative small scale. Like the choice of colors, the quilt's pattern is unusual, consisting of a small central floral appliqué design surrounded by eight identical fernlike plumes that curve around the central design's four spiking corners, and eight crowns that are evenly spaced at the quilt's corners and midpoints. The plumes and crowns are also appliquéd in place. The crowns are clearly intended to represent those worn by Hawaiian monarchs, although the crosses on the tops of the crowns have been greatly enlarged and stylized for design purposes. To provide further variety in the quilt's overall design, the four corner crowns differ slightly from the four set at the quilt's midpoints. Interrupted bands instead of single solid bands frame their centers, and the area below the bands is also subtly different from the corresponding area in the other four crowns.

The medium intensity purple fabric chosen for all the appliqué pieces is also used for the quilt's binding, which was sewn in place with a sewing machine. The entire quilt is covered with carefully sewn contour stitching which echoes the forms of the seventeen appliqué pieces that make up the overall design.

Hawaiian Islands. Cottons, hand appliquéd and quilted. 82 ½ x 81 ½ in.
Honolulu Academy of Arts, Honolulu. Gift of Mrs. Charles M. Cooke Estate.

Ke Kahi O Ka'iulani

[THE CROWN OF KA'IULANI]

Artist unknown · Early 20th century

This stunning quilt honors Princess Victoria Ka'iulani, the niece of Queen Lili'uokalani. The English-educated princess, daughter of a Hawaiian mother and a British father, had been appointed by Lili'uokalani to be her successor to the throne when she was only fifteen. She was greatly admired by the Hawaiian people and was considered by many to represent the last and best hope for Hawaiian sovereignty. Unfortunately, the princess suffered frail health, which was destined to dash that dream. This quilt was made shortly after her untimely death from rheumatic fever in 1899 at the age of twenty-four, just a year after the annexation of the islands by the United States. Ka'iulani's tragic passing was deeply mourned by the Hawaiian people, both because she was a beloved and romantic figure and because it signaled the end of any realistic chance for the restoration of the monarchy. As a measure of respect, she was buried in the Royal Mausoleum beside Hawaii's former kings and queens.

The complex pattern represents the princess's hair combs, which are embellished with crowns and leaf leis. Eight-pointed stars are cut into the tops and bottoms of the plume-shaped combs, and small five-pointed stars are placed at either side of each comb. Eight larger five-pointed stars are set within the field of the central design and another eight at the quilt's outside corners and midpoints; these undoubtedly represent the eight major islands of Hawaii. A large eight-pointed star forms the center of the quilt and is echoed by the smaller star cut out of its heart. The many cut-outs open the pattern up by balancing the red appliqué and white background, keeping the viewer's eye moving back and forth between the contrasting colors. The rather plain quilting is done by machine in straight lines that intersect to form a grid of one-inch squares over the entire surface of the quilt.

Above: Detail of top eight-pointed star design.
Right: Island of Hawaii. Cottons, hand appliquéd, with machine quilting. 88 1/2 x 84 in.
Honolulu Academy of Arts, Honolulu. Gift of Mrs. Richard A. Cooke.

Embroidered Annexation Quilt

Kelliʻiahonui Richard · 1910

This early twentieth-century quilt is decorated with embroidery stitches rather than the more commonly seen cutout appliqué pattern. The design is built on repetitions of the Hawaiian coat of arms. This coat of arms includes both the royal Hawaiian flag and a stylized rendition of the American flag, with a single star in its field. The paired flags patriotically proclaim the island's new affiliation and symbolize unity between the territory and its new government. Made a dozen years after the Hawaiian Islands were annexed by the United States, the quilt sets eight full coats of arms around the unwreathed central medallion.

The maker of this quilt appears to have been pleased with the annexation, a sentiment not shared by most Hawaiians at the time. Although these peace-loving people gave up any thought of revolt after the arrest of Queen Liliʻuokalani in 1895, antigovernment feeling lingered for years. Hawaiians had great pride in their former monarchy and monarchs, this attachment evidenced by the continuing tradition of the royal Hawaiian flag quilt. It is not surprising, therefore, that relatively few quilts that incorporate American flags into their design exist, and those that do include the flag do not appear to have been imitated by other quilters.

The word *Aloha,* stitched on the banner at the top of the coat of arms, is the best-known word in the Hawaiian language. It is also perhaps the most complex, used to convey many things—hello, goodbye, love, farewell—and suggests a full range of emotions—joy, hope, sadness, loss. To Hawaiians, these meanings are neither contradictory nor mutually exclusive, and all were undoubtedly intended to resonate here.

Kelliʻiahonui Richard was the great-grandmother of contemporary Hawaiian quiltmaker Elizabeth Akana's husband. Like most of Hawaii's patriotic quilts, hers has been lovingly preserved and handed down within her family.

Above: Detail of coat of arms design.
Right: Oahu. Cottons, hand embroidered and quilted. 76 x 72 in. Collection of Elizabeth Akana.

Hawaii Ponoi

[HAWAII'S OWN]

Artist unknown · c. 1880

Nani Ahiahi

[BEAUTIFUL EVENING]

Artist unknown · c. 1915

While almost all existing flag quilts date after the 1893 coup that deposed Queen Lili'uokalani, and none are documented earlier than 1880, Hawaiian quilt historian Elizabeth Akana has argued that the form may have been made as early as 1843, when the islands were claimed for the crown by the British naval commander Lord George Paulet. Paulet acted during a land dispute between the British consul and King Kamehameha III, fearing that France might take over the islands. His decision was ultimately reversed by the British crown. However, during the five months before the islands were returned to the king, Paulet ordered that all Hawaiian flags that could be found be destroyed, a move that affected the citizens of the islands deeply. Akana speculates that Hawaiians, realizing for the first time how vulnerable their kingdom and its revered symbol were, may well have been prompted to construct quilts that incorporated the forbidden flag into their designs. Such quilts would have served as surrogates for the flag and as emblems of a secret keeping of faith with the usurped kingdom.

Early flag quilts probably would have been copied when they were threatened by the islands' destructive climate. These two atypical examples may be copies of much earlier quilts. The words *Hawaii Ponoi,* meaning "Hawaii's own," refer to the flags; this quilt carries only a single crown framed by crossed laurel branches. *Nani Ahiahi* means "beautiful evening," perhaps metaphorically referring to the end of the Hawaiian kingdom. This quilt's central medallion consists of a representation of the earliest Hawaiian coat of arms, which was adopted in 1845 and considerably altered in 1883. It is possible that the design dates as far back as the adoption of the coat of arms, and probable that it was first made before 1883.

Above: Hawaii Ponoi (Hawaii's Own). Artist unknown. c. 1880. Hawaiian Islands.
Cottons, hand pieced, appliquéd, and quilted. 72 x 74 in. Private collection.
Right: Nani Ahiahi (Beautiful Evening). Artist unknown. c. 1915. Hawaiian Islands.
Cottons, hand pieced and quilted. 78 x 78 in. Mission Houses Museum, Honolulu.

Anthurium

Mary Manoi · 1912–30

Anthurium is one of the signature flowers of Hawaii, outranking even orchids in popularity among the islands' florists. The plant's long stems are topped with bright red waxy flowers accented by protruding yellow stamens. The spectacular flowers hold extremely well after cutting, making them ideal for commercial and household use.

This quilt was assembled in 1912 but was not completed until 1930, when the contour quilting was added. While most Hawaiian floral designs move from the center outward, this quilt's unusual design reverses that standard pattern. The center of the quilt is left open, placing visual emphasis on a wide outer border instead. The quilt lacks a central motif; it is, in effect, all border, which acts as a ground from which eight anthurium plants grow toward the quilt's center. Large flowering anthuriums spring from each

of the quilt's corners and are complemented by smaller plants set in the middle of each side.

Although modern quilters have expanded the palette of Hawaiian quilts, the use of four colors was extremely uncommon in traditional Hawaiian appliqué quilt design. Most early Hawaiian quilts employed only two colors, and only a few are known to have been made with three or more. The simple color schemes in Hawaiian quilts resulted from two related factors: adherence to tradition and limited access to fabric choices. Most traditional patterns were designed for two colors, so if a quilter wanted to use more, she usually had to come up with an original pattern. Mary Manoi clearly felt that the colorful flowers of the anthurium deserved to be captured, so she devised a pattern that would allow her to add color accents to the basic green-on-white palette of the quilt.

Maui. Cottons, hand appliquéd and quilted. 91½ x 84 ½ in. Private collection.

Awapuhi

[RED GINGER]

Artist unknown · c. 1930

This quilt was given to Dr. Charles S. McGill in 1930 in appreciation for his treatment of a young Hawaiian who showed symptoms of infantile paralysis. At the time, Dr. McGill was the doctor for the Olaa Sugar Plantation on the big island of Hawaii and also worked out of the Hilo Memorial Hospital. He nursed the boy through his illness, and after his recovery the family presented Dr. McGill with the quilt. The boy's mother had originally intended it as a wedding gift for her son, but the family felt that the quilt was small thanks indeed for what they regarded as Dr. McGill's gift of the boy's life.

Awapuhi or Hawaiian ginger *(Zingiber zerumbet)* is native to the islands. The plant grows from a rhizome, which produces a one- to three-foot stem carrying about a dozen leaves arranged in opposing vertical rows. The plant is often called shampoo ginger because, when squeezed, the stems yield a liquid that has long been used as a hair treatment. In earlier times, its leaves were used to flavor roasted meat, especially pork.

Despite the ginger plant's familiarity, it has inspired relatively few quilt designs. Researcher Stella Jones noted in 1930, "Even the common plumeria and the humble morning glory have been used as motifs for quilt designs [but] the only ginger quilt I've seen was designed on Kauai." In recent years, however, researcher Elizabeth Akana has seen six patterns similar to the one used for this quilt.

The range of plants that have served as inspiration for Hawaiian quilts is nearly as broad as the islands' diverse flora itself. A list compiled by Stella Jones of patterns she had seen includes fuchsia, fig, mango, sunflower, chrysanthemum, carnation, hot chili pepper, pomegranate, grapes, coconut, pineapple, breadfruit, banana, guava, trumpet flower, lily of the valley, Mexican creeper, prickly pear, and an assortment of lilies and roses.

Island of Hawaii. Cottons, hand appliquéd and quilted. 78 x 69 in. Collection of Dr. C. S. McGill.

Kukui O Lono

[LAMP OF LONO]

Maria Namahoe Kelley · c. 1921
Assisted by Adele Kelley and Meali'i Namahoe

This quilt was a collaboration between Maria Namahoe Kelley and her daughters, Adele, aged ten, and Meali'i, aged thirteen. The quilt was made as a gift for Mrs. Kelley's son, the girls' brother. The intricate lacy design is believed to have been inspired by decorative lamps at the entrance of Kukui O Lono Park on Kauai.

Meali'i, whose married name was Kalama, grew up to become Hawaii's best-known and most honored quiltmaker. This quilt, which stands apart on its aesthetic merits, is thus also historically important, placing Kalama's well-known later work into its formative, family context. In Hawaii as in the United States, quiltmaking was most often learned by doing. Mothers like Mrs. Kelley gave their daughters progressive lessons in sewing and designing patterns and before having them try a quilt on their own, enlisted their help with their own projects. Mothers coached their daughters through the different steps of crafting a quilt, making suggestions whenever help was needed with the more difficult tasks, such as the elaborate and time-consuming quilting of the surface. In this way girls gained pride, experience, and confidence as well as the cherished memory of working with their mother on an enjoyable and creative project. These memories often became a driving force in a woman's later quiltmaking, as each new quilt became a means of reconnecting with her mother's spirit. These feelings of spiritual kinship, which lie at the heart of Hawaiian quiltmaking, were only deepened if, as was often the case, one's grandmothers and great-grandmothers were also quilters. And the intimacy inherent in the quilt was further strengthened when it was made as a gift for a loved one.

This quilt is one of the many that have been documented by the Hawaiian Quilt Research Project, a nonprofit organization which has explored and recorded the islands' quiltmaking heritage since its founding in 1990.

Honolulu, Oahu. Cottons, hand appliquéd and quilted. 87 x 77 in. Private collection.

Bird of Paradise

Alice Mahelona · c. 1925

This quilt was made by Alice Mahelona for Margo Armitage when Margo was a young girl. Mrs. Mahelona was a professional needleworker who teamed with Margo Armitage's aunt in a dressmaking venture. Margo Armitage Morgan grew up to be an outstanding quiltmaker in her own right.

The addition of a number of small, appliquéd tricolored flowers between the center and border motifs brightens and enlivens the quilt's highly stylized design. The unusual combination of Jazz Age colors, including jade green, lemon yellow, pink, and dark blue, probably reflects the wide range of cotton fabrics available to a professional dressmaker in the 1920s. The quilt is backed with a sheet of bright pink fabric.

Few island quiltmakers had the luxury of employing such elegant contemporary fabrics in their work. Early Hawaiian quiltmakers made resourceful use of whatever fabric was available to them. Relatively inexpensive cotton bedsheets were often used as backgrounds for appliqué, and two or more large pieces of fabric were sometimes carefully sewn together to make up a quilt top when a single large sheet could not be found or afforded.

Backings, which were not intended to be seen, were often made of rough fabric, such as muslin, and occasionally several pieces of fabric were sewn together to make up the backing. One known flag quilt has a backing comprised of nine-patch piecework clearly rummaged from discarded scraps. Contrary to conventional wisdom, many quiltmakers used printed fabrics as well as solid colors for their appliqué patterns. The deciding factor seems to have been efficacy: if printed fabric was at hand, it was used. Calicos with small prints were common in the islands and turn up in older quilts with some degree of frequency. Many of these small prints have faded over time and can appear to be solid colored if they are not inspected carefully.

Above: Detail of center design.
Right: Hawaiian Islands. Cottons, hand appliquéd and quilted. 83 x 79 in.
Mission Houses Museum, Honolulu. Gift of Margo Armitage Morgan.

Unnamed Floral Pattern

Artist unknown · c. 1930

Although most Hawaiian quilts are square, this example was made in a slightly elongated shape to accommodate its unusual overall design. The central design fits within a square. However, the quiltmaker decided to extend the design to fit a rectangular shape. To fill out the corners of the rectangle, the quilter has added an almost complete, nearly exact mirror image of the floral design unit that repeats four times to form the interlocking central pattern. The unexpected rhythms resulting from the large negative (white) spaces at the centers of the sides give the quilt part of its visual interest, as do the four complex negative shapes repeated in the quilt's center. Together, the four small negative shapes at the center of the quilt make up a strong crosslike form, which is set with its points and helps to balance the larger off-point rhythm of the overall pattern.

Note that the middles of the buds at the top center of the corner units are cut out, while they are left uncut in the four central design units, and that the long flowering branches that flank each of the central units have been omitted from the corner designs. The centers of the flowers of the larger designs are also cut out, while those of the corner units are not, and the pairs of stems flanking the corner units' buds are without side shoots. All these slight modifications add interest to the complex and dainty pattern of the quilt by upsetting the eye's expectations as it scans the repeating designs.

Square formats were ideally suited to the large cutout appliqués favored by Hawaiian quiltmakers. The precisely symmetrical patterns were far more difficult to plan and execute in the rectangular format than in the square.

Hawaiian Islands. Cottons, hand appliquéd and quilted. 92 x 84 in. Collection of Susan Parrish Antiques.

Flower Vase of the ('Iolani) Palace

Mary Kaulahao · c. 1930

'Iolani is Hawaiian for "Bird of Heaven." The design for this quilt was inspired by the etched urn pattern on the glass doors of 'Iolani Palace in Honolulu. 'Iolani Palace was built by King Kalakaua, a man of considerable ego who felt the existing palace, a modest house also called 'Iolani, was not nearly grand enough for him. Work on the new palace was begun in 1879; it took almost four years and over $300,000 to complete and furnish. In addition to its etched glass doors, the extravagant king's new royal residence featured columned galleries, gold-framed mirrors, heavy red velvet draperies, and a seven-foot royal bathtub made of marble. Kalakaua celebrated his move into the completed palace by spending another $50,000 on a coronation, even though he had been king for nine years by that time. He was invested amid the grandest pomp and circumstance, and was presented with the feather cape of King Kamehameha I and a new jeweled gold crown he placed on his own head. French and American warships fired salvos from Honolulu harbor, a choir sang the newly composed anthem "Cry Out O Isles with Joy," and the royal band played Meyerbeer's "Coronation March." The celebration party following the coronation lasted two weeks and included fireworks, a regatta, and a luau for five thousand guests.

While the foreign investors who essentially controlled the islands thought the whole extravaganza indecorous at best, native Hawaiians, in whose eyes Kalakaua could do no wrong, loved every minute of it. They were inordinately proud of the palace as well, which to them represented the glory of Hawaii and its royalty. This quilt embodies the strong nationalist feelings of most Hawaiians of the period, who correctly feared their islands and their sovereignty would ultimately be wrested from them by the foreigners.

Oahu. Cottons, hand appliquéd and quilted. 90 x 84 in. Collection of Lyman House Memorial Museum.

Unnamed Floral Pattern

Artist unknown · c. 1930

In most Hawaiian quilts, a dark-colored appliqué pattern dominates the light-colored field on which it is sewn. If the designer did cut through the darker material to reveal the lighter color background underneath, the cut-outs were usually small and only accented the larger pattern. This quilt's dynamic appliqué cut-out, however, creates a pattern that combines positive (blue-on-white) and negative (white-on-blue) designs of equal size and strength. Two almost identical enclosed large half-circular white-on-blue designs fill the sides of the quilt's central X shape and create a powerful visual pulse at the quilt's center. Although these abstract designs are created out of vegetable forms, they are masklike in effect, with pairs of blue flowers seemingly placed to suggest animal or human facial features that are reminiscent of early Hawaiian religious wood carvings.

Early Hawaiians believed that the physical world was made up of paired opposites, and this basic philo-sophical tenet profoundly affected their approach to quilt design. In the introduction to her translation of the ancient Hawaiian genealogical chant called the *"Kumulipo,"* Martha Beckwith makes a statement that can be applied to this quilt's pattern, which is made up of pairs of designs that alternate around a central focus: "[The Hawaiian] arrives at an organized concept of form through the pairing of opposites, one depending on the other to complete the whole. . . . Ideas of night and day, light and darkness, male and female, land and water, rising and setting (of the sun), small and large, hard and light (of force), upright and prostrate, upward and downward, toward and away, appear paired in repeated reiteration as a stylistic element in the composition of chants, and functions also in everyday language, where one [of the] pair lies implicit whenever its opposite is used in reference to the speaker."

Hawaiian Islands. Cottons, hand appliquéd and quilted. 78 ½ x 75 in. The Shelburne Museum, Shelburne, Vermont.

Pikake and Tuberose

Hannah Kuʻumililani Cummings Baker · 1938

Hannah Kuʻumililani Cummings Baker (1906–1981) was the key figure in keeping traditional quiltmaking alive in Hawaii during the middle decades of the twentieth century. During this period, traditional Hawaiian quiltmaking declined drastically under pressure from the many new people and cultural influences that flooded the Hawaiian Islands before and after World War II. Hannah Baker began making quilts in the 1920s and remained active into the 1970s, providing a bridge between the old traditions and their revival in the 1960s. This lovely, lacy quilt is typical of Baker's best work, combining a strong central design with a complex, complementary border and detailed contour quilting.

Throughout her long career, Baker collected and shared many traditional patterns and also designed many of her own original patterns. In addition she lectured widely about Hawaiian quilts and taught thousands of students during her thirty-year career as a quilting instructor. Her great desire was to share the art of the Hawaiian quilt with as many other quilters as possible. To that end, copies of the 213 patterns she designed and collected were donated to the Bishop Museum by her family after her death. The Hawaiian Quilt Research Project will soon begin documenting the entire Baker collection and will ultimately expand its availability by placing copies of some of the patterns in other public institutions.

Although Hawaiian quilters traditionally shared patterns, not all island quilters have been as generous with their patterns as Hannah Baker. Some guard their own or their families' designs jealously and refuse to let others copy them. Because of the recent growth of interest in traditional quiltmaking, patterns now have commercial value and are sold to eager quiltmakers on and off island.

Honolulu, Oahu. Plain woven cotton, hand appliquéd and quilted,
with machine-stitched edging. 86 x 86 in. Bernice Pauahi Bishop Museum, Honolulu.

Unnamed Floral Pattern

Artist unknown · c. 1940

Red on white is the most common color scheme found on traditional Hawaiian floral quilts. Early quilt designers found that setting red cut-outs on a white background allowed the appliqué design to stand out boldly and cleanly. White backgrounds were also popular for more practical reasons: white cotton bedsheets were often used as quilt tops because they were widely available and relatively inexpensive.

Economy was undoubtedly one determining factor in the evolution of the Hawaiian quilt; the islanders' aesthetic preferences went hand in hand with their thriftiness and the efficient use of materials. Hawaii's climate did not require many garments, and most native clothing styles were made from large, simply cut pieces of fabric. Similarly, it was far cheaper to craft a quilt from two large pieces of cloth than to cut into several different pieces of fabric to create varied colors and patterns. This fact probably explains the relative rarity of three-color quilts in the Hawaiian

tradition, since few early quiltmakers could justify the expense of a third piece of fabric, especially if it was to be used simply as an accent.

This bold red-on-white design sets a large cross shape at the center of the quilt and adds V-shaped forms, suggestive of potted plants, in the four corners. A small, negative white diamond at the very center is echoed by the overall form of the central design. The cross shape is filled out with a repeating pattern of four smaller floral designs set on and within a linear framework that makes up a four-pointed star. While the name of the overall pattern is unknown, the quilt-maker most certainly had a name for it. Unlike their mainland counterparts, Hawaiian quilters rarely signed or marked their work. Names of designs were, however, often marked on paper patterns that were passed down, like quilts themselves, within families. Paper patterns that have survived in museums and in private collections can often help to identify lost design names.

Hawaiian Islands. Cottons, hand appliquéd and quilted. 85 x 81 in. Collection of Ardis and Robert James.

Ka Ua Kani Lehua

[THE RAIN THAT RUSTLES LEHUA BLOSSOMS]

Artist unknown · 1940–50

The lehua is one of Hawaii's most common trees. It is particularly prevalent on the Big Island, where it grows as tall as one hundred feet. The tree has gray bark and gray-green leaves that provide a muted background for its bright red, pomponlike flower clusters. Early Hawaiians believed that the fire red blossoms of the lehua were sacred to Pele, the powerful and temperamental goddess who controls the islands' volcanoes. They also believed that if one picked a lehua blossom it would rain.

Lehua blossoms are among those most commonly used for leis, the garlands made of flowers, hair, leaves, nuts, shells, or other natural objects that have been made and worn by Hawaiians for centuries. Early Hawaiians identified themselves with particular natural objects and often wore or gave leis made from their personal totems. In his book *Man, Gods and Nature,* Michael Kioni Dudley explains, "Hawaiians saw themselves as reflecting nature, and viewed all of nature, including the cosmos itself, as reflecting them. . . . The Hawaiians' world was filled with sentient beings which formed an interrelating community with them. They depended upon, cared for, and communicated with the surrounding world of nature, and it depended on, provided for, protected, and communicated with them . . . Many, if not most, Hawaiians still have a general orientation in which they experience nature as distantly related kin."

Handmade leis were considered among the most precious of gifts, and each carried the symbolic meanings of its flowers to the recipient. Leis also have traditionally marked rites of passage in Hawaiian life: even today, births, christenings, graduations, marriages, anniversaries, and even deaths are occasions for their exchange. In recent years, floral leis have, of course, become a cliché in the tourist industry, which has often trivialized their historic and interpersonal meanings. Still, the typical tourist's visit to the islands is not complete without a lei and an *Aloha,* both of which retain the power to rise above their commercialization and endure as sincere gifts of the islands.

Hawaii. Cottons, hand appliquéd and quilted. 84 x 78 in. Private collection.

'Ahinahina

[SILVERSWORD]

Junedale Lauwaeomakana Quinories · 1961

'Ahinahina

[SILVERSWORD]

Rebecca L. Muraoka · c. 1946

Silversword is a gray-green plant that grows primarily inside the huge crater of the volcanic Mount Haleakala on the island of Maui. The plant's dozens of thin leaves form a round bushlike shape that grows up to two feet around. Silversword, thought to have descended from ancient seeds of wind-blown California tarweed, is a desert plant that has adapted itself specifically to withstand the extreme weather conditions found in the otherwise barren crater of the volcano, where rainfall is minimal and sun-baked days are followed by nights of bitter cold. The plant's name comes from its knife-shaped leaves, which are covered with shiny hairs that reflect moisture-robbing sunlight. The narrow leaves store water in a gelatinlike material that fills the spaces between the plant's cells. The silversword grows for as long as fifty years without blooming, then produces a single spectacular flower spike and dies after flowering. The spike, which can rise as high as eight feet, is covered with hundreds of bright magenta flowers. This unusual plant has become endangered in recent years

by Argentine ants, whose arrival on Maui illustrates some of the unpredictable effects of foreign influence on Hawaii's ecology. The insects, which reached the crater in the 1960s, are predators of a native bee that pollenates the silversword.

The traditional pattern used for both of these quilts depicts the silversword in its typical nonflowering state. Contrasting approaches to color and quilting distinguish the two. Rebecca L. Muraoka, who made her quilt from her great-grandmother's pattern, chose a rich and unusual combination of colors that show off the graphic pattern to great effect. Junedale Quinories quilted her starker red-and-white bedcover with a turtle's back pattern, a traditional Hawaiian stitching motif that complements the plant forms of the design perfectly. Although the quilting pattern was named for its resemblance to the shells of sea turtles, the turtle-backs here suggest leaves or flower buds and add a textural layer of floral forms to the surface of the quilt that more conventional contour quilting does not provide.

Above: 'Ahinahina (Silversword). Junedale Lauwaeomakana Quinories. 1961. Mountain View, Island of Hawaii.
Cotton/polyester, hand appliquéd and quilted. 97 x 97 in. Collection of the artist.
Right: 'Ahinahina (Silversword). Rebecca L. Muraoka. c. 1946. Kauai.
Cottons, hand appliquéd and quilted. 91 x 90 in. Collection of Meryl and Christopher Lewis.

Coconut and Pineapple

Meali'i Kalama · 1973

eali'i Kalama is considered one of the greatest of Hawaiian quilt designers. This quilt's simple but striking original design, typical of her work, demonstrates why she is so highly regarded by other island artisans. The design employs the two most immediately recognizable of Hawaiian plants, the coconut palm and the pineapple. Using only three forms—a palm tree with coconuts, a large pineapple, and a small pineapple—each repeated eight times, Kalama built a powerful design full of undulating curves that are reinforced by the quilting. The strong graphic design can be understood at a glance, but it also includes many subtle elements that become apparent on careful scrutiny.

Coconuts were brought to the islands by the Polynesians, who planted groves of them near their seaside villages. Early Hawaiians used coconuts for dozens of different purposes: the fruits provided both food and drink, empty coconut shells became cups and containers, husks were made into rope and thread for sewing, and palm fronds were woven into baskets and mats. Hawaiian homes were built on coconut-trunk foundations, roofed with coconut-frond thatch, and sited in the shade of nearby palms.

Pineapples, a South American fruit, were growing wild in the islands as early as the 1790s, although it is unclear how they got there. They may have been introduced by Captain Cook, who is known to have brought them to several other South Pacific island groups. However, because many of the fruits spoiled when shipped and tended to ferment and explode when canned, pineapples were not a significant crop in Hawaii during the nineteenth century. The key figure in the rise of the pineapple as a Hawaiian crop was James D. Dole, who arrived in Hawaii in 1899 and singlehandedly brought the fruit to prominence in the island's agriculture. He solved the canning problem and through clever and widespread advertising raised public interest in the previously little-known pineapple. In 1922 Dole bought most of the island of Lanai, which is still known as the "Pineapple Island," and covered it with pineapple farms to meet the burgeoning world demand he had created. Today, pineapples are closely identified with Hawaii and rank with sugar cane as the most important crop of the islands.

Honolulu, Oahu. Cotton/polyester, hand appliquéd and quilted. 108 x 108 in. Private collection.

Flower Garden

Meali'i Kalama · c. 1988

eali'i Kalama was named a National Heritage Fellow by the National Endowment for the Arts, Folk Arts Program in 1985. She is the only Hawaiian quilt-maker who has been given an award by the program, which honors living masters of traditional arts. This splendid example of her work was acquired by the International Folk Art Foundation, which owns representative pieces by most of the National Heritage "folk masters."

Meali'i Kalama (1909–1992) was taught quiltmaking by her grandmother. Like many Hawaiian quilters, Kalama's first quilt was a breadfruit pattern, which she made at the age of thirteen under her grandmother's supervision. Kalama was an extremely important advocate for the traditional Hawaiian quilt. Through her teaching in the 1960s and 1970s, she exerted a profound influence on a new generation of quilters who are continuing the tradition she helped to save. Among her protégées is Elizabeth Akana, a leading quiltmaker, teacher, and researcher in the islands today.

Kalama's work has been widely exhibited around the world and has introduced many to the beauty of traditional Hawaiian quiltmaking. In the mid-1960s, Kalama was asked by Laurence Rockefeller to make thirty quilts for his luxurious Mauna Kea Beach Hotel on the island of Hawaii, built as a sanctuary for business leaders. Her quilts have also been the subject of museum exhibitions and have probably been seen by more people than the work of any other island quiltmaker.

Meali'i Kalama offered these thoughts about quiltmaking, which apply to all Hawaiian quilts: "I cannot quilt when I am troubled or under stress. I make mistakes and must undo the work. I make quilts with loving thoughts of the persons who will receive and use the quilts. Quilting requires clean thoughts as well as clean hands. You would not want a quilt that was soiled by dirty hands and you would not want a quilt which was not made with love."

Honolulu, Oahu. Cottons, hand appliquéd and quilted. 89 x 81 in. International Folk Art Foundation Collection, Museum of International Folk Art, a unit of the Museum of New Mexico, Sante Fe, New Mexico.

Lokelani

[ROSE OF HEAVEN]

Mattie Stevens Smith · c. 1920

Lokelani

[ROSE OF HEAVEN]

Lois Joslyn Smith · 1985

Quiltmaking was traditionally an activity shared by grandmothers, mothers, and daughters within a Hawaiian family, and patterns were often passed down through the generations. These two quilts were made from the same pattern, which has descended through three generations of the Smith family. Lois Joslyn Smith is married to one of Mattie Stevens Smith's grandsons and inherited a family collection of sixty quilt patterns gathered by Mattie Smith and her daughter-in-law, Jennie Uaia Smith, with whom Lois quilted.

Lois Joslyn Smith learned Hawaiian quilting from her mother-in-law, Jennie; Lois's grandmother, Mele Uaia, was also a quiltmaker. Although Lois Joslyn Smith was born into a Pennsylvania German family, her marriage to Jennie's son piqued her interest in Hawaiian traditions, including quiltmaking. Jennie's daughter showed no interest in quiltmaking, so Jennie basted a quilt for each of her daughters-in-law to see which of them might be interested in continuing the family tradition. Lois appliquéd and quilted

her first quilt in 1980 and has continued making quilts following the family patterns ever since.

According to Lois Joslyn Smith, "Jennie Uaia Smith kept the family's Hawaiian traditions alive through language, music, storytelling, and quilts. The beginnings of Hawaiian quilts lie in the memories of women no longer here to tell us. Each island has its own legends, its own music, its own quilt patterns, named for winds, for rains, for plants. The traditions depend on the memories of the children and grandchildren. Too many tales have been forgotten. We were very lucky that Grandma and her family remember so many of those stories. There is a warmth created by those grandparents which will always be remembered."

The floral design used for these two quilts combines roses with silversword in the corners. Lois Joslyn Smith has simplified and stylized the original pattern, but her quilting is far more intricately worked than Mattie Smith's, which is not contoured.

Above: Lokelani (Rose of Heaven). Mattie Stevens Smith. c. 1920. Kohala, Hawaii.
Cottons, hand appliquéd and quilted. 75½ x 78½ in. Collection of Lois Joslyn Smith.
Right: Lokelani (Rose of Heaven). Lois Joslyn Smith. 1985. San Jose, California.
Cottons, hand appliquéd and quilted. 98 x 97 in. Collection of the artist.

Ka Hasu Nani O Hale'iwa

[THE BEAUTIFUL LOTUS OF HALE'IWA]

Doris Iwalani Feary Nosaka · 1984–86

This large and unusual quilt, which is an original design, employs a rare combination of three fabric colors to suggest flowering lotuses floating in a pond. The solid field of dark mossy olive green represents the murky pond water, while the leaves of the lotus are worked in a light greenish blue and accented with soft lavender pink flowers. The four small corner blocks and the square inner border which frames the central floral pattern are design elements often used by mainland American quiltmakers but almost never found in Hawaiian quilts. The geometric frame here suggests an enclosure for a man-made lily pond, its lines providing a striking contrast to the flowing curves of the appliqué pattern. Traditional contour quilting, suggestive of ripples on a pond, fills the quilt top. The leaves, buds, and flowers are accented with stitches that complement their shapes, adding a soft, third textural dimension of natural form to the design.

Doris Nosaka learned Hawaiian quiltmaking from Meali'i Kalama and other earlier masters of the art and has been active for years as a teacher and organizer of quilters' groups. This quilt's design was inspired by a lotus pond in Hale'iwa on the island of Hawaii, where Doris Nosaka lives. This pond in turn evoked memories of the extensive lotus ponds on an estate owned by Princess Ruth Ke'elikolani, where Doris Nosaka often visited as a child.

The cultivated lotus or water lily has been a favorite of Oriental gardeners and artists for centuries and may have been brought to Hawaii by Chinese or Japanese immigrants. The lotus flourished in the tropical climate of the islands, and many of the grand estates built by foreign businessmen and native royalty in Hawaii during the nineteenth century included ponds full of lotuses among their formal gardens.

Island of Hawaii. Cottons, hand appliquéd and quilted. 103 x 101 in. Collection of the artist.

'Ahinahina O Haleakala

[THE SILVERSWORD OF HALEAKALA]

Annette Sumada · 1986

The volcano Haleakala is Maui's tallest peak, towering 10,000 feet above the island and 25,000 feet above the ocean floor from which it rose to create the larger, eastern part of the island. The volcano last erupted around 1790, and many believe that it will become active again in the next one hundred to two hundred years. The volcano's crater is enormous (7 ½ miles long, 2 ½ miles wide, and ½ mile deep), an arid moonscape that Jack London described as "a scene of vast bleakness and desolation, stern, forbidding . . . a workshop of nature cluttered with the raw beginnings of world-making."

Haleakala, which means "House of the Sun," is the primary home of the silversword plant, which grows in the crater's desert climate. Trade winds dump 250 inches of rain on Haleakala's eastern side annually, creating spectacular waterfalls and lush forests, but are spent of moisture by the time they reach the summit. The mountain and rain forest below it are a national park, preserving thousands of acres of astonishing natural beauty and offering protection to the silversword and a host of other rare and exotic plants and birds. Thanks to the efforts of Laurence Rockefeller, Charles Lindbergh, and other prominent and powerful conservationists, East Maui is one of the least developed regions of Hawaii, providing a model for careful, nonexploitative use of the islands' natural resources.

This quilt's central design depicts four intersecting silversword plants, their long flower spikes in full bloom. Plants with shorter flower spikes are at the center of each of the quilt's sides, and plants with spikes about to burst into flower are in each corner. Pairs of small nonflowering plants flank their larger cousins around the edge of the quilt, while small mound shapes set between each plant may represent the volcano itself.

Island of Hawaii. Plain woven cotton, hand appliquéd and quilted. 110 x 110 in. Collection of Jiro Alan Sumada.

Me Kealoha O Kaua ʻOhana Wahihanai

[WITH LOVE FOR OUR FAMILY RANCH]

Junedale Lauwaeomakana Quinories · 1987–89

In an interview with researcher Elaine Zinn, the quiltmaker talked about the origin and meaning of this quilt: "My husband wanted me to design a quilt for our ranch. And so I thought about it and thought about it. One day we were driving out the coast and I was smiling. and he looked at me and he said, 'Well, what are you smiling about?' I said, 'I got it.' I drew the design and I put the horseshoe inside, which is about the horses that belong to my husband. And the *kuni* [branding iron] in the middle. And then around it has *maile,* which is the love for the ranch. And because we are surrounded by lehua on three sides of our ranch, I designed two haku leis surrounding it. And then in each corner, I put the *puʻu oʻo* [lava] which is Pele [the volcano] showing how she's flowing down to the lehua trees and into the forest. She brings down the heat . . . She is heating up that branding iron so

we are able to brand the cows we have on the ranch. All of this truly is my 'expression of love' for our family ranch."

Junedale Quinories' mother was a professional quiltmaker who also made bedcovers for her family. Quinories worked with her mother as a young girl, helping her baste and stitch appliqué designs in place, after which her mother did all the quilting. She did not begin quilting herself until after the birth of her first child, for whom she and her mother each made a quilt. Each of her other five children have also received a quilt made by their mother. Although this quilt is an original design, most of Quinories' quilts follow traditional patterns. She prefers the old patterns because they remind her of her mother, whose spirit continues to bring special meaning to her quilting.

Above: Center design detail of the horseshoe and *kuni.*
Right: Designed 1987. Completed 1989. Mountain View, Island of Hawaii.
Cotton/polyester, hand appliquéd and quilted. 108 x 108 in. Collection of Adam Quinories.

Ylang-Ylang

Margo Armitage Morgan · 1986

Many Hawaiian quilts embody special memories and feelings, which are often known only to the quiltmaker. This quilt evokes a typically complex chain of associations and emotions stretching back to the artist's childhood and linking friends past and present, living and departed, through the image of a beloved flower. According to Margo Morgan, "The pattern [for the quilt] was given to me in friendship, reminding me of a special friend, now deceased, who brought me the ylang-ylang blossoms when we were in grammar school. She knew I loved the fragrance and thoughtfully shared [them with me]."

Margo Armitage Morgan is a highly respected Oahu quiltmaker who works from traditional patterns that have been given to her over the years. This quilt's wide and intricately contoured outer border, which includes a number of small plant forms, is a design solution rarely found in Hawaiian quilts. Typically, the quilt's floral design would have been framed in a square, resulting in far more open white space, and outlined only by the narrow strip of binding fabric that edges the quilt. This quilt has, in effect, four borders that frame the central motif, which, in typical Hawaiian fashion, is formed of a floral form mirrored at right angles in each quadrant of the quilt. First, the central motif is encircled by a thin, almost square garland of floral forms that echoes the smaller circle at the center of the quilt. Next comes a white space decorated with a series of plumes which extend from the outside of the garland. Third is the wide outer border, and finally the square blue binding. The entire design, from the central circle of flowers to the outmost border, can be broken into mirroring quadrants, and the whole surface of the quilt is covered with intricate contour stitching which echoes the main elements.

Honolulu, Oahu. Cottons, hand appliquéd and quilted. 110 x 110 in. Collection of the artist.

Volcano Quilt: I Ka Ho'okumu Ana
[IN THE BEGINNING]

Helen Friend · 1989

While most Hawaiian quilt designs are based on indigenous plant forms, this unique contemporary example reaches to the islands' primordial past to evoke the volcanic explosions that first lifted Hawaii out of the waters of the Pacific and have continued to reshape the islands throughout their history.

Helen Friend says, "I see [the volcano] as the birth of the island. This chain of islands is here because of the power of the volcano." Her original design places the viewer in a godlike position, looking down into the volcano from high above. Depicting streams of molten lava as they pour down a mountainside from the mouth of an erupting volcano, the quilt's stylized image is totally unlike most Hawaiian designs in its impact. It is violent rather than peaceful, active rather than passive, dramatic rather than subdued, and direct rather than subtle. The intense contrast of the red-on-black color scheme is also unique among Hawaiian designs, which usually place strong colors like red on a neutral background, such as white or cream.

The quilt is also uncommon in its use of reverse appliqué, which is one of Friend's specialties. Instead of being cut from a piece of cloth that is then sewn onto the quilt's surface, the appliqué design here was cut out of the black cloth, which is the top layer, to reveal the red underneath. The reverse-appliqué method is particularly appropriate to this quilt's design because it suggests the physical reality of lava spewing out of the earth and cutting riverbeds into the land over which it runs.

Although the subject matter, color scheme, and technique of this quilt are unusual, its basic pattern was created in the traditional Hawaiian fashion, by cutting a piece of folded cloth to achieve a radiating, symmetrical design.

Honolulu, Oahu. Cottons, reverse-appliquéd and quilted. 96 x 96 in. Persis Collection, *Honolulu Advertiser Newspaper.*

Kualoa

[BREADFRUIT]

Helen Friend · 1992

Breadfruit was the most important of all indigenous South Pacific food plants. It was carried throughout the region by ancient Polynesian sailors, who planted the breadfruit tree wherever they landed. In early Hawaii it ranked just behind sweet potatoes and taro in favor. The breadfruit's English name, most likely assigned to it by someone who had never seen the tree or tasted its fruit, is puzzling and misleading. Breadfruit is closer to a starchy vegetable than a fruit and bears no resemblance to bread other than its high carbohydrate content. The breadfruit tree bears a round fruit that grows six to eight inches in diameter, each fruit a "composite" actually made up of thousands of small berrylike fruits that grow together. The fruit is cooked before eating; it can be boiled, fried, or baked as a sweetened pudding.

Helen Friend made this quilt as a wedding present for her daughter. The solid green center of the quilt is stitched with concentric circles, one for each year of the friendship between the newly wedded couple.

Male and female flowers also appear in the center; the male flowers form the initials "MW," for Mary Williamson, the bride's married name. Kualoa, which is near the site of the wedding, was one of the first landing spots on Oahu for the early Polynesian voyagers who discovered and settled the Hawaiian Islands. Helen Friend chose to create a breadfruit pattern for the quilt because of the tree's connection with the ancient sailors who planted it at Kualoa and because of its place in Hawaiian mythology as a sustainer of life.

Helen Friend is a certified midwife and textile artist who was born in England and emigrated to Hawaii in 1966. She has been "a passionate needlewoman" all her life and discovered quiltmaking "as an expression" in 1985. She says, "Quilting is to me a most satisfying way of recording my life. My ideas come first, then a color choice appropriate to the emotion. I am not a traditional Hawaiian quilter; as quilting is so labor-intensive, I find no time or reason to copy traditional patterns."

Honolulu, Oahu. Cottons, hand appliquéd and quilted. 96 x 96 in. Private collection.

Hapuʻu

[TREE FERN]

Rachel P. Keehne and Malia Range Keehne · 1989–91

Rachel Keehne was born in Honolulu and is of Hawaiian, Chinese, German, Irish, French, and Indian ancestry. She studied Hawaiian quiltmaking with Doris Nosaka and has created a number of innovative new designs. Her mother, Malia, who made this quilt following Rachel's design, is a florist. The complex quilt contrasts the strong central forms of four crossed tree trunks with a background of delicately cut and colored foliage.

Hapuʻu are tree ferns native to Hawaii. They tolerate either wet or dry climates and grow into dense fern forests in many parts of the islands. At higher elevations they grow twenty feet tall and can have three-foot trunks topped with fronds that are twelve feet long. Ancient Hawaiians used pulu, the silky fluff that covers the fronds, as an absorbent for wounds and as an embalming material, and Hawaiian quiltmakers sometimes used it as batting.

Rachel Keehne writes, "If you were to walk up to a tree fern, [you would see a] chocolate-brown trunk with curled immature buds tightly bound in furry but silky fuzz. Overhead would extend a light-green canopy of lacy fronds that seemed delicate but strong. This quilt was designed because other hapuʻu designs did not express the lacy frond effect I tried to capture. The trunk and leaves were matched as closely as possible to the actual fern in color. The background had to be rather dark to [set off] the mint-green fronds. Peach was selected because it allowed both trunk and fronds to be clearly shown.

"We hope [our] quilt will portray this forest fern long after man has bulldozed our forest for farms or homes. Better still, we hope Hawaii will always have deep forests filled with hapuʻu where birds sing and build their nests and the sound of rain keeps [the] fronds glistening like so many prisms that become thousands of rainbows!"

Designed by Rachel P. Keehne, made by Malia Range Keehne. Keaau, Island of Hawaii.
Cottons, hand appliquéd and quilted by Malia Range Keehne. 107 x 102 in. Collection of Malia Range Keehne.

Hawaiian Police Heritage Quilt

Elizabeth Akana · 1992

This modern flag quilt was commissioned by the Honolulu Police Department in celebration of its sixtieth anniversary. The quilt's central medallion traces the history of law enforcement in Hawaii through a series of emblems and badges arranged chronologically. In early days feather helmets were worn by lesser chiefs who enforced the laws set by the ruling chief. Later, the Hawaiian government's "Organic Acts" of 1845–47 created the office of marshall of the kingdom, a position which assumed the duties of the islands' chief law-enforcement officer. The acts also provided for a subordinate sheriff on each of the four major islands. These offices remained in place until 1900, when the office of marshall was dissolved and replaced with a territorial high sheriff's office. In January 1932 the Honolulu Police Department (represented here by its original star-shaped badge) replaced the local territorial sheriff's office there. The other islands soon followed suit.

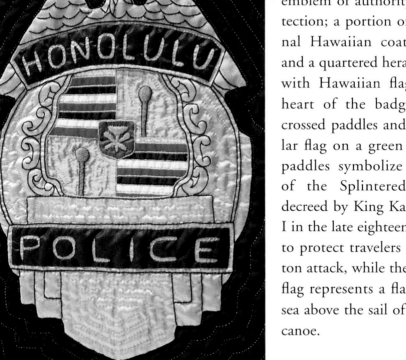

In the late 1940s a new, shield-shaped badge was designed for the Honolulu Police Department by a retired detective, Alfred Karratti. Like this quilt, it incorporated design motifs spanning the history of the police in Hawaii. Seen here are the kapu stick, an ancient emblem of authority and protection; a portion of the original Hawaiian coat of arms; and a quartered heraldic device with Hawaiian flags. In the heart of the badge are two crossed paddles and a triangular flag on a green field. The paddles symbolize the "Law of the Splintered Paddle," decreed by King Kamehameha I in the late eighteenth century to protect travelers from wanton attack, while the triangular flag represents a flag raised at sea above the sail of the chief's canoe.

On traditional flag quilts the top flag flies upside down, but Elizabeth Akana wanted to avoid this symbol of distress (or even disrespect) and placed all the flags on this quilt in an upright position.

Above: Detail of central shield.
Right: Oahu. Chintz, satin, and imperial broadcloth, appliqué and feather work by Elizabeth Akana, embroidery by Harriet Yamaguchi, quilting by Kathie Dallas. 71 x 71 in. Collection of the Honolulu Police Department.

Jonathan/My Way

Elizabeth Akana · 1992

Elizabeth Akana has created several two-sided quilts with interlocking appliqué and quilted designs that add to and reinforce each other's impact and meanings. Instead of having a top and a back or underside, these quilts have, in effect, two equally important tops: the quilting on the one side repeats the appliqué forms on the other. Each side stands on its own, but when taken together they add up to a third, greater whole.

This double-sided quilt was inspired by Richard Bach's best-selling novel *Jonathan Livingston Seagull,* the inspirational story of a bird who dares to stray from the flock. One side of Akana's quilt depicts Jonathan flying with the flock, while the other shows him proudly flying alone. The quilting on each side reminds the viewer of the unseen part of the story. Jonathan's quilted form can be seen above the

appliquéd flock on one side, and the quilted flock is seen below an appliquéd Jonathan on the other. Thus Jonathan and the flock are literally intertwined in the fabric of the quilt. According to Elizabeth Akana, "This quilt . . . reminds us all to be all that we can be, that indeed we do not have to fly with the flock but can instead be our own bird."

Elizabeth Akana is widely considered to be Hawaii's foremost contemporary quiltmaker, researcher, and teacher. She wrote *Hawaiian Quilting: A Fine Art* and is, with filmmaker Elaine Zinn, the founder of the Hawaiian Quilt Research Project. She was born in New Jersey but has lived in Hawaii since the mid-1960s. There she continues her love affair with the Hawaiian quilt, at once delving deeper into its history and meanings and expanding its future through her own creative designs.

Above: Reverse of quilt showing seagull with the flock.
Right: Kaneohe, Oahu. Chintz and iridescent taffeta, quilted by Kathie Dallas. 68 x 58 in. Collection of the quiltmaker.

Ayame'

[IRISES]

Sharon Balai and Dorothy Satsue Hamada · 1995

This quilt represents the combined design talents of two outstanding modern Hawaiian quiltmakers. According to Sharon Balai, "[I designed] the original pattern in 1990 for a king-size bed quilt. I named it Ayame', which means 'Iris' in Japanese, to honor Japanese women in our Ka Hui Kapa Apana O Waimea quilt club. Their dedication and craftsmanship [helps] keep Hawaiian quilting alive. The iris flower bears special significance to women of [Far Eastern] ancestry. Mrs. Hamada, who is of Japanese ancestry, discovered the pattern in the organization files and was touched by the dedication. After making numerous quilts for others, she decided this was the quilt she would make for herself. However, the pattern didn't fit her bed, so at her request I reduced it to queen size and added a border. The flower garden full of colors was her own compositional idea."

Hawaiian quiltmakers have often adapted or combined patterns to suit their own needs or express their own feelings. Adding a border or using different color combinations are the most common ways of changing a pattern. The mid-twentieth-century quiltmaker, designer, and pattern collector Hannah Ku'umililani Cummings Baker was famous (or notorious) for combining parts of older patterns and forming new wholes, often adding a border of her own design to dress up a simple older pattern she had collected. Because these types of alterations are part of the ongoing creative and organic folk process that is Hawaiian quiltmaking, they are rarely documented by their makers, and only in recent years have researchers begun to sort out where one quilt design ends and another begins. Patterns are also often renamed when taken up by another quilter, a practice that can further obscure their origins and history.

Dorothy Hamada was born in Waimea on the island of Hawaii and studied Hawaiian quiltmaking with Doris Nosaka. She is a prolific quiltmaker who has contributed many of her works to benefit community organizations on Hawaii.

Designed by Sharon Balai, adapted and made by Dorothy Satsue Hamada. Kamuela, Hawaii.
Cottons, hand appliquéd and quilted. 96 x 84 in. Collection of Dorothy Satsue Hamada.

Kuʻu Aloha Me Piʻiana

[MY EVER INCREASING LOVE]

Sharon Balai · 1993

This delicately colored quilt represents the Orchid or Butterfly tree of the Bauhinia family and was made for the quiltmaker's oldest daughter, whose Hawaiian name is Kuʻualoha. It speaks of love for her and for Hawaiian quilting. According to Sharon Balai, "This was my second attempt at [designing] a large quilt. Although the Orchid tree is not a native and was recently introduced to Hawaii, it enjoys our climate and does well here. The blossoms are a striking magenta against a pale bluish green. The tree made quite an impression on me when I first saw it. I thought it was the most beautiful combination I'd seen. This quilt expresses my initial amazement and awe that is so much like the love for your first born."

Sharon Balai, who first took up Hawaiian quiltmaking in 1985, is president of Ka Hui Kapa Apana O Waimea, the Hawaiian quilting club of Waimea. The group, which meets monthly, was established in 1972 and has members not only from the island of Hawaii but also from the other islands in the state of Hawaii, as well as mainland United States, Canada, Japan, Australia, and France.

"We are unique—the largest original Hawaiian quilting club promoting the spirit of *Aloha* in helping others to learn and to perpetuate the art," Balai states proudly. The membership includes a number of master quilters who are very active designing and producing original quilts. The group maintains a collection of over two hundred designs and holds quilt shows every two years that feature a minimum of twenty new quilts. How-to sessions are a regular feature at the shows. The club provides the expertise and materials for these sessions as well as for special community programs, hotel cultural activities, local schools, and craft fairs.

Kamuela, Hawaii. Cottons, hand appliquéd and quilted. 102 x 102 in. Private collection.

Kiele Onaona

[FRAGRANT GARDENIAS]

Sharon Balai · 1994

Sharon Balai explains the creation and personal meaning of her quilt in this way: "My home . . . is at about 9,000 foot elevation and the climate is cool and misty. The temperatures range from the upper 30s to the lower 80s. Gardenias [are] one of my favorite flowers, do especially well here and grow in profusion all around my home. *Kiele Onaona* . . . is my third attempt at making a Hawaiian quilt and conveys my appreciation for the special way their fragrance surrounds and encompasses you into pleasant relaxation at the end of a day. This quilt was made for my second daughter whose Hawaiian name translates to mean 'beautiful flower.'"

Balai adds, "Upon completion of this quilt, I was surprised to find that I actually prefer the appearance of the stitched design from the back." Her unusual quilt is in effect two quilts in one: a Hawaiian appliqué on one side and an elaborately quilted whole cloth on the other.

Elizabeth Akana, whose own double-sided quilts are so masterfully stitched, has pointed out that all quilts are in a sense double sided, and that the back can sometimes hold as much or more interest than the front or "top" of a quilt. The top is made to be seen and admired; it is the decorative part of the quilt and therefore carries the pieced or appliquéd design, which is usually embellished with complementary quilted patterns sewn either by hand or by machine. The reverse or "back," which is most often made from a single piece of monochromatic, plain-colored cloth, shows off the stitching. Except in the case of a whole cloth quilt, where the only decoration on the solid-colored top is stitching, quilting is almost always secondary to pattern in both impact and intent. For this reason, any quilt will be better appreciated if viewed not only from the top but also from the back, where its quilting can be examined apart from the pattern.

Above: Reverse side of quilt.
Right: Kamuela, Hawaii. Cottons, hand appliquéd and quilted. 100 x 96 in. Collection of the artist.

Na Pua E Liko Aniani

[FLOWERS AND BUDS MIRRORED]

Stan Yates · 1994

Stan Yates is one of the most innovative of contemporary Hawaiian quiltmakers and designers. He has brought a number of fresh ideas to traditional Hawaiian appliqué design and continues to experiment with "all the components of the design that can be varied, juxtaposed or utilized for visual effect." He continues, "I learned Hawaiian quiltmaking about nine years ago from my then-spouse, who was born and raised on the island of Oahu, where she learned Hawaiian quilting as a teenager from her grandma and aunties. By the time we married, she had completed perhaps ten quilts, mostly full-size and she was quite expert at appliqué. [However,] her rather marked astigmatism made it difficult for her to quilt evenly and one day when she expressed consternation, I offered to quilt a row or two. I haven't stopped since."

In creating his own patterns, Yates has applied his love of the complex geometric art of the Dutch artist M.C. Escher to Hawaiian quilt design, developing what he calls "double designs," which are built of a single floral shape that repeats in both foreground and background. According to Yates, "The key aspect of the double quilt design is that the symmetry of its unit cell can be shifted at its outer edge so that when outer edges of two unit cells are joined, the 'outside' becomes the 'inside.' The unit cell fits a 22 $1/2$-degree radial segment, so two unit cells comprise the standard 45-degree segment that yields the traditional eight-fold Hawaiian quilt design."

Yates specializes in baby and crib-size quilts, most of which are used as wall hangings by their owners, but hopes to create double designs to fit full-size quilts as well. He is currently working on a design for a round quilt that will include "palm trees, dolphins leaping, and cresting sea waves" and hopes to learn to create "mitered" corners that join two oblique surfaces.

Eleele, Kauai. Cottons, hand appliquéd and quilted. 44 x 44 in. Collection of Mr. and Mrs. C.F. Story.

Malapua Pilialoha

[FRIENDSHIP GARDEN]

Cathy Estess · 1994

This striking quilt is notable for its strong, stylized central design of large, spade-shaped anthurium blossoms and for its bold and unusual pink-on-black color scheme. The anthuriums are surrounded by a border of Cup of Gold, a trailing vine with huge flowers that grows wild throughout upland areas near the quiltmaker's home, and by a scalloped outside edge of plain pink, representing the sea surrounding the islands, "both isolating and uniting them." The distinctive stamens of the anthurium flower are represented by thin curved strips of white fabric which are appliquéd onto the pink blossoms. The gently curving lines of the anthurium stems, blossoms, and stamens are set in a variety of different orientations that give the entire center of the quilt a sense of slow but constant organic motion, almost as if the flowers were growing out and over each other.

The anthurium blossoms are cleverly arranged into inner and outer rows with stems emanating from a circle at the quilt's center. Eight blossoms make up the inner group, while the outer row contains sixteen flowers. A subtle eight-pointed star is cut into the central circle in relief so that it shows in black; the eight thin lines defining the star are similar in width to the white stamens. These lines also reveal the design's precise underlying symmetry, since when drawn out by the eye they are seen to divide the entire quilt into its basic structural components and design elements.

Cathy Estess was born in San Francisco in 1926 and moved to Hawaii in 1987. A needleworker since childhood, she took up Hawaiian quiltmaking soon after arriving in the islands and has been an active member of the Big Island's Ka Hui Kapa Apana O Waimea quilting group for many years. Of this quilt she says, "The combination of elements to me symbolizes the unity and diversity of Hawaii, where many cultures meet and blend into a harmonious whole. This is the Hawaii I have come to know and love, a place of warmth and acceptance—a Malapua Pilialoha."

Kailua-Kona, Hawaii. Cottons, hand appliquéd and quilted. 102 x 102 in. Collection of David and Elaine Estess.

Index

Photo Credits

Photo courtesy America Hurrah: p. 16.
Photo courtesy American Quilter's Society: photo by Richard Walker: p. 67.
Photo by Ken Burris: pp. 27, 75.
Photo Field Museum, Chicago: neg. no. A104033c: p. 34.
Photo courtesy Rod Kiracofe: photo by Tom Vinetz: p. 63; photo by Sharon Risedorph: p. 83.
Photo courtesy Kokusai Art: front cover, pp. 31, 34, 35, 37, 55, 56–7, 77, 82, 91, 93, back cover.
Photo by Paul Komada, Honolulu: pp. 29, 49, 51, 61, 68–9, 99.
Photo by Tibor Pranyo © Honolulu Academy of Arts, Honolulu: pp. 14, 23.
Photo by Don Queralto: p. 12
Photo by Sharon Risedorph: pp. 25, 58–9, 60, 65, 88, 89, 95, 97, 103, 109, 111, 112–13, 115, 117.
Photo by Ron Testa: neg. no. A106376c: p. 32; neg. no. A109505c: p. 33.
Photo by Turner and DeVries: pp. 41, 81.
Photo by Shuyo Uemoto: p. 20.